JAMESTOWN EDUC

 M000314002

Reading Science

Strategies for English Language Learners

Intermediate

 Glencoe

New York, New York   Columbus, Ohio   Chicago, Illinois   Peoria, Illinois   Woodland Hills, California

JAMESTOWN EDUCATION

Image Credits: Cover (prism)ThinkStock, (satellite)CORBIS,
(globe)Creatas, (others)Getty Images.

Glencoe

The *McGraw·Hill* Companies

Copyright © 2006 by The McGraw-Hill Companies, Inc. All rights reserved. Except as
permitted under the United States Copyright Act of 1976, no part of this publication may
be reproduced or distributed in any form or by any means, or stored in a database or
retrieval system, without prior written permission of the publisher.

Send all inquiries to:
Glencoe/McGraw-Hill
8787 Orion Place
Columbus, OH 43240-4027

ISBN 0-07-872915-7 (Student Edition)
ISBN 0-07-874225-0 (Teacher Edition)

Printed in the United States of America.

1 2 3 4 5 6 7 8 9 10 066 11 10 09 08 07 06

Contents

Reading is one of the fastest ways for you to get information. *Reading Science* can help you improve the way you read and understand science topics. You will also learn how to improve your test-taking skills.

Before You Read

These steps can help you *preview* an article and get an idea of what it is about.

Read the title. Ask yourself "What can I learn from the title?" and "What do I already know about this subject?"

Read the first sentence or two. The writer wants to catch your attention in the first sentence or two. You may also find out what you are about to learn.

Skim the entire article. Look over the article quickly for words that may help you understand it. Jot down unfamiliar words in your Personal Dictionary. You can ask someone later what they mean.

Participate in class discussions. Your teacher may show you pictures or objects and ask you questions about them. Try to answer the questions.

While You Read

Here are some tips to help you make sense of what you read:

Concentrate. If your mind wanders, remind yourself of what you learned when you previewed the article.

Ask yourself questions. Ask yourself "What does this mean?" or "How can I use this information?"

Look for the topic of each paragraph. Each paragraph has a main idea. The other sentences build on that idea. Find all of the main ideas to understand the entire article.

Refer to the vocabulary you have learned. The words in dark type will remind you of what you learned in the Vocabulary section. For more help, refer to the previous page.

After You Read

The activities in *Reading Science* will help you practice different ways to learn.

A. Organizing Ideas Webs, charts, and tables will help you organize information from the article. Sometimes you will create your own art.

B. Comprehension Skills will help you recall facts and understand ideas.

C. Reading Strategies will suggest ways to make sense of what you read.

D. Expanding Vocabulary will teach you more about the vocabulary you learned before and during reading.

Vocabulary Assessment

After every five lessons, you can try out what you have learned. Activities, such as postcards and advertisements, show you how the vocabulary can be useful and fun in everyday life. Enjoy!

Pronunciation Key

a   as in *a*n or c*a*t

ä   as in *fa*ther or *a*rm

ā   as in m*a*de, s*ay,* or m*ai*d

e   as in w*e*t or s*e*ll

ē   as in h*e*, s*ee*, m*ea*n, n*ie*ce, or lov*e*ly

i   as in *i*n or f*i*t

ī   as in *I,* m*i*ne, s*igh*, d*ie,* or m*y*

o   as in *o*n or n*o*t

ō   as in f*o*ld, b*oa*t, *ow*n, or f*oe*

ô   as in *o*r, *oa*r, n*augh*ty, *aw*e, or b*a*ll

oo   as in g*oo*d, w*ou*ld, or p*u*t

ōō   as in r*oo*f or bl*ue*

oi   as in n*oi*se or j*oy*

ou   as in l*ou*d or n*ow*

u   as in m*u*st or c*o*ver

ū   as in p*u*re, c*ue*, f*ew,* or f*eu*d

ur   as in t*ur*n, f*er*n, h*ear*d, b*ir*d, or w*or*d

ə   as in *a*while, mod*e*l, sec*o*nd, or col*u*mn

f   as in *f*at, be*f*ore, bee*f,* stu*ff,* gra*ph,* or rou*gh*

g   as in *g*ive, a*g*ain, or do*g*

h   as in *h*at, *wh*ole, or a*h*ead

k   as in *k*itchen, boo*k,* mo*ck,* or *c*ool

l   as in *l*ook, a*l*ive, hee*l*, ta*ll,* or fo*ll*ow

m   as in *m*e, i*m*agine, or see*m*

n   as in *n*o, i*n*side, in*n*ing, or fu*n*

ng   as in si*ng*er, bri*ng,* or dri*n*k

p   as in *p*ut, o*p*en, or dro*p*

r   as in *r*un, fo*r*m, or wea*r*

s   as in *s*ocks, her*s*elf, or mi*ss*

sh   as in *sh*ould, wa*sh*ing, or ha*sh*

t   as in *t*oo, en*t*er, mi*tt*en, or si*t*

th   as in *th*ink, no*th*ing, or too*th*

t̲h̲   as in *th*ere, ei*th*er, or smoo*th*

v   as in *v*ote, e*v*en, or lo*v*e

w   as in *w*ell or a*w*ay

y   as in *y*ellow or can*y*on

z   as in *z*oo, ha*z*y, or si*z*es

zh   as in sei*z*ure, mea*s*ure, or mira*ge*

N   as in *bonjour* (vowel before the **N** is nasal)

KH   as in *loch* (or German *ach*)

Before You Read

Tip! **Think about what you know.** Skim the article on the opposite page. What do you know about space travel? Try to find out which country was the first to put a person on the Moon.

Vocabulary

The content-area and academic English words below appear in "The History of Space Travel." Read the definitions and the example sentences.

Content-Area Words

rocket (rok′it) a machine that burns fuel and mixes it with air to make hot gases that push it through the air
Example: The simplest *rocket* is the kind used for fireworks.

calculations (kal′kyə lā′shənz) math work, such as addition or multiplication
Example: His *calculations* in math class were almost always correct.

altitudes (al′tə tōōdz′) heights above Earth's surface
Example: High *altitudes* scare me, so I do not travel in the mountains.

satellite (sat′əl īt′) a vehicle that circles heavenly bodies, such as Earth or the Moon
Example: The scientists built a *satellite* that sent back pictures of the planet Venus.

orbits (ôr′bits) moves in a circle around (something)
Example: Just as the planets circle the Sun, the space station *orbits* Earth.

Academic English

goal (gōl) an accomplishment toward which effort or work is directed
Example: My *goal* was to clean my room today, and I did it!

cooperated (kō op′ə rat′əd) acted with another or others for a common purpose
Example: A group of students *cooperated* to do a class project.

Complete the sentences below that contain the content-area and academic English words above. Use the spaces provided. The first one has been done for you.

1. We say that the planets *orbit* the Sun because they circle it _____ .
2. The family *cooperated* to change the tire by _____ .
3. The student finished the *calculations* by _____ .
4. That space vehicle must be a *satellite* because it _____ .
5. The plane rose to high *altitudes* when it _____ .
6. In the race, the finish line was our *goal* because _____ .
7. We could see that *Saturn 5* was a *rocket* because _____ .

 Dictionary Now skim the article and look for other words that are new to you. Write each new word and its definition in the Personal Dictionary.

While You Read

 Think about why you read. Have you ever worked with someone to get a job done? As you read, look for the paragraph about countries working together in space.

THE HISTORY OF
Space Travel

1 For centuries people dreamed of going into space. This dream began to seem possible when high-flying rockets were built in the early 1900s. A **rocket** travels through the air by shooting out hot gases. Burning fuel produces these gases.

In 1903 a Russian teacher named Konstantin Tsiolkovsky figured out how
5 to use rockets for space travel. His plan was the first one in rocket science to use correct scientific **calculations.** About 30 years later, a U.S. scientist named Robert Goddard built the first rockets that could reach high **altitudes.** In Germany in the 1920s, Hermann Oberth wrote a book that helped people understand that the new rockets made it possible to fly to space. During World
10 War II, German scientists built large rockets that could travel very far and carry dangerous explosives. After the war, scientists from Germany went to the United States and the Soviet Union to help those countries build space rockets.

These two countries were soon racing to get to space first. Each of these countries wanted to prove that it was stronger and more advanced than the
15 other one. Both countries also had powerful bombs. Because these bombs used hydrogen fuel, they were called hydrogen bombs. People in the United States were worried when the Soviets were first to launch a space **satellite,** which was called *Sputnik.* The Soviets were also first to send a person into space. Yury Gagarin orbited Earth in the *Vostok 1* spaceship in 1961.

20 The U.S. government set as a **goal** for its space program to be the first country to put a person on the Moon. The U.S. space program built a series of Apollo spaceships. These vehicles were powered by huge *Saturn 5* rockets. In 1969 *Apollo 11* took three men to the Moon. Neil Armstrong became the first person to walk on the Moon.

25 The Soviets may have lost the race to fly people to the Moon, but they built the first space station. The United States also built a space station. The space stations allowed people to live and work in space. Then the Soviet Union and the United States **cooperated** to hook two spaceships together in space. This action ended their "space race." Today a much larger space station, built by
30 several countries together, **orbits** Earth.

Another new way to travel in space is by space shuttle. A space shuttle looks like an airplane. Astronauts, or men and women who fly spaceships, have used shuttles to help put satellites into space. They have also helped build space stations and have worked on scientific experiments.

LANGUAGE CONNECTION

Synonyms are words that have the same or similar meanings. The words *move* and *journey* are synonyms for *travel.* Can you think of a synonym for the word *built?*

CONTENT CONNECTION

In the 1960s, the United States built a *series* of spaceships. The series was made up of several Apollo spaceships that were similar and were used one after another. How is the World Series of baseball games similar to the series of Apollo spaceships?

After You Read

A. Organizing Ideas

What happened in space travel during the 1900s? Complete the time line below with dates and facts. Reread the article, and look for the dates of important events in the history of space travel. Write the dates on the lines. In the box below each date, write an important fact about that date. The first one been done for you.

Time Line of Space Travel

Early 1900s

High-flying rockets were built.

How did this time line help you as you learned dates and information about space travel? Write two or more sentences about one of the dates you recorded on the time line.

_____

_____

_____

_____

_____

_____

B. Comprehension Skills

 Think about how to find answers. Look back at what you read. The information is in the text, but you may have to look in several sentences to find it.

Mark box **a, b,** or **c** with an **X** before the choice that best completes each sentence.

Recalling Facts

1. The first person to build high-altitude rockets was
   - ☐ **a.** Neil Armstrong.
   - ☐ **b.** Hermann Oberth.
   - ☐ **c.** Robert Goddard.

2. The two countries in a "space race" were
   - ☐ **a.** the Soviet Union and the United States.
   - ☐ **b.** Germany and the United States.
   - ☐ **c.** the Soviet Union and Germany.

3. The first person to travel in space was
   - ☐ **a.** Neil Armstrong.
   - ☐ **b.** Yury Gagarin.
   - ☐ **c.** Hermann Oberth.

4. The spaceship that carried the first person to land on the Moon was
   - ☐ **a.** *Sputnik.*
   - ☐ **b.** *Vostok 1.*
   - ☐ **c.** *Apollo 11.*

5. The space station that is currently orbiting Earth was built by
   - ☐ **a.** several countries.
   - ☐ **b.** the United States and the Soviet Union.
   - ☐ **c.** Japan and Germany.

Understanding Ideas

1. From the article, you can conclude that space travel would not have been possible without the invention of
   - ☐ **a.** the space shuttle.
   - ☐ **b.** rockets.
   - ☐ **c.** *Skylab.*

2. Americans probably were worried about *Sputnik* because
   - ☐ **a.** it seemed that the Soviets had better scientists.
   - ☐ **b.** they thought that *Sputnik* might be full of bombs.
   - ☐ **c.** there were no U.S. rockets.

3. From the article, you can conclude that the tools for living in space have
   - ☐ **a.** gotten old and slow.
   - ☐ **b.** been a total waste of money.
   - ☐ **c.** led to the development of satellites.

4. People probably thought that it would be important for people to live and work in space because
   - ☐ **a.** scientists had not been sure how long people could survive in space.
   - ☐ **b.** it meant that we could stop exploring space.
   - ☐ **c.** we could see photographs of the planets for the first time.

5. This article suggests that
   - ☐ **a.** the United States won the "space race."
   - ☐ **b.** the Soviet Union won the "space race."
   - ☐ **c.** both the United States and the Soviet Union made the dream of space travel come true.

C. Reading Strategies

1. Recognizing Words in Context

Find the word *hook* in the article. One definition below is closest to the meaning of that word. One definition has the opposite or nearly the opposite meaning. The remaining definition has a meaning that has nothing to do with the other two words. Label the definitions **C** for *closest,* **O** for *opposite* or *nearly opposite,* and **U** for *unrelated.*

_____ **a.** connect

_____ **b.** separate

_____ **c.** choose

2. Distinguishing Fact from Opinion

Two of the statements below present *facts,* which can be proved. The other statement is an *opinion,* which expresses someone's thoughts or beliefs. Label the statements **F** for *fact* and **O** for *opinion.*

_____ **a.** The United States put the first person on the Moon.

_____ **b.** Germany had the best rocket scientists in the world.

_____ **c.** The Soviet Union put the first satellite into space.

3. Making Correct Inferences

Two of the statements below are correct *inferences,* or reasonable guesses, that are based on information in the article. The other statement is an incorrect, or faulty, inference. Label the statements **C** for *correct* inference and **I** for *incorrect* inference.

_____ **a.** It took a long time and a lot of work to send a person into space.

_____ **b.** Studying space and visiting space were important goals for many countries.

_____ **c.** Russians make better astronauts than Americans do.

4. Understanding Main Ideas

One of the statements below expresses the main idea of the article. Another statement is too general, or too broad. The other explains only part of the article; it is too narrow. Label the statements **M** for *main idea,* **B** for *too broad,* and **N** for *too narrow.*

_____ **a.** *Sputnik* was the name of a Soviet satellite.

_____ **b.** The work of scientists and astronauts from all over the world has allowed people to explore space.

_____ **c.** Rockets help many types of spaceships get to space.

5. Responding to the Article

Complete the following sentences in your own words:

One of the things I did best while reading "The History of Space Travel" was

_____

I think that I did this well because _____

_____

D. Expanding Vocabulary

Content-Area Words

Read each item carefully. Write on the line the word or phrase that best completes each sentence.

1. Rockets travel into space by burning _____.
   electricity   fuel   water

2. Scientists have to do many calculations in order to _____.
   train astronauts   plan space travel   set up a government

3. If you fly at a high altitude, you are _____ Earth's surface.
   above   at   below

4. The Soviet satellite, called _____, was the first in space.
   Shuttle   *Spider*   *Sputnik*

5. A large _____, which has astronauts living and working
   in it, orbits Earth.
   space station   space shuttle   rocket

Academic English

In the article "The History of Space Travel," you learned that *goal* means "an accomplishment toward which effort or work is directed." *Goal* can also mean "an aim or a purpose," as in the following sentence.

   My goal is to become a better trumpet player.

Complete the sentence below.

1. The *goal* of a doctor is to _____

Now use the word *goal* in a sentence of your own.

2. _____

You also learned that *cooperated* means "acted with another or others for a common purpose." *Cooperated* can relate to countries that worked together. *Cooperated* can also relate to other people and things that worked together, as in the following sentence.

   Science and history teachers cooperated to create lessons about inventions.

Complete the sentence below.

3. Members of the soccer team *cooperated* in order to _____

Now use the word *cooperated* in two sentences of your own.

4. _____

5. _____

 Share your new sentences with a partner.

Before You Read

 Think about what you know. Do you know what a botanist does? If not, read the title and the first line of the article on the opposite page to help you figure out what a botanist may do.

Vocabulary

The content-area and academic English words below appear in "What Is a Botanist?" Read the definitions and the example sentences.

Content-Area Words

taxonomy (tak son′ə mē) the organization of animals and plants into groups according to their features
Example: Taxonomy helps us understand differences between classes of plants and animals.

characteristics (kar′ik tə ris′tiks) features, such as size and color, that identify someone or something
Example: Green skin and black spots are *characteristics* of some frogs.

bred (bred) caused to reproduce or grow
Example: The woman *bred* roses to sell at a local market.

environment (en vī′rən mənt) surroundings that affect life and growth
Example: Dirty water is not a healthful *environment* for fish.

ecology (ē kol′ə jē) the study of the relationship between a living thing and the world around it
Example: Ecology explores how changes in weather and air quality affect animals and plants.

Academic English

transport (trans pôrt′) carry from one place to another
Example: My job is to *transport* boxes of books to the library by truck.

research (rē′surch′) careful search or examination
Example: His long hours of *research* resulted in an accurate and detailed paper.

Read again the example sentences that follow the content-area and academic English word definitions. With a partner, discuss the meanings of the words and sentences. Then make up a sentence of your own for each word.

 Now skim the article and look for other words that are new to you. Write each new word and its definition in the Personal Dictionary.

While You Read

 Think about why you read. A *botanist* is a scientist who studies plants. What else do botanists do? As you read, try to find the answer to this question.

What Is a Botanist?

1 Botany is the science of plants. A plant is a living thing that cannot move by itself. A plant also has no nervous system. This means that it has no brain or nerves.

A botanist is a scientist who studies plants. Some botanists identify plants and place them into groups. Their work is called plant **taxonomy.** Botanists classify plants into
5 groups according to the parts of the plants. There are two main groups, or *phyla,* of plants. One *phylum* is made up of plants that are more complex than other plants. These are called vascular plants. They have parts that **transport** water and food through the plant. Some examples of vascular plants are trees, herbs, and shrubs.

The second group, or phylum, is made up of simpler plants that do not have
10 true roots, stems, or leaves. They are called nonvascular plants because they do not have special parts to move water and food. Two examples of nonvascular plants are mosses and liverworts. The two plant phyla are divided into many smaller groups of plants.

Throughout history botanists have learned about plants by studying them,
15 or doing **research.** They have learned how green plants make their own food, how the tiny cells inside a plant work, and how plants reproduce. In the 1600s, a British scientist named Robert Hooke used one of the first microscopes to look closely at plant parts. He learned that plants have cells. Later, people learned that all living things have cells. An Austrian monk named Gregor Mendel, who lived
20 in the 1800s, studied how plants pass on **characteristics** to other plants. He **bred** pea plants that looked different from one another. When the new plants grew, he carefully recorded what they looked like. He noticed how they were like or unlike the plants that they were bred from. Then he wrote down his ideas.

Some botanists study plant fossils to learn about what our planet was like
25 many years ago. A fossil is an outline or a shape left in rock by a dead plant or animal. Plants appeared on Earth before animals did, so the oldest fossils are plant fossils. Knowing what kinds of plants lived in an area can tell scientists what the **environment** was like. If scientists find fossils of ocean plants in an area that is now a desert, they know that there was once an ocean in that place.

30 Botanists do many other kinds of work. Some teach at schools. Some study how plants can be used to make medicines. Others work to grow new types of crops, or plants that can be useful to people or animals. A botanist might develop a strain of corn that insects do not like to eat. Botanists also work in forests, where they help develop new trees. Botanists work in the field of **ecology** to study how
35 plants are affected by environment.

CONTENT CONNECTION

The main idea of this article is that botanists study plants in different ways. The second paragraph tells readers how botanists use plant taxonomy to classify plants. The fifth paragraph shows how studying fossils helps botanists reach conclusions. What kinds of research are described in the fourth paragraph?

LANGUAGE CONNECTION

The noun *strain* (in line 33) refers to a group of animals or plants that have certain characteristics. A *strain* of corn means a "kind" of corn. Why would a new strain of virus be a problem?

After You Read

A. Organizing Ideas

What jobs do botanists do? Complete the web below. In each circle, record something that botanists do. Refer to the article to help you. The first circle has been done for you.

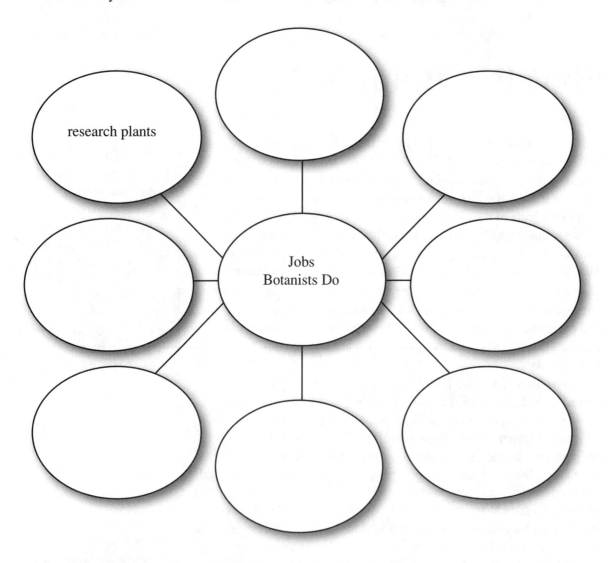

What does this web show you about the work botanists do? Write two or more sentences that describe the job that is most interesting to you. When you learn about something new, how do you like to organize the new information? Explain your answer.

_____

_____

_____

_____

B. Comprehension Skills

 Think about how to find answers. Think about what each sentence means. Try to say it to yourself in your own words before you complete it.

Mark box **a**, **b**, or **c** with an **X** before the choice that best completes each sentence.

Recalling Facts

1. All plants are living things that
   - ☐ **a.** have parts that move water and food.
   - ☐ **b.** are unable to move around by themselves.
   - ☐ **c.** leave fossils in layers of rock.

2. The science of classifying plants into groups is called
   - ☐ **a.** ecology.
   - ☐ **b.** heredity.
   - ☐ **c.** taxonomy.

3. Botanists organize plants into groups according to the plants'
   - ☐ **a.** height.
   - ☐ **b.** color.
   - ☐ **c.** parts.

4. The oldest fossils are from
   - ☐ **a.** plants.
   - ☐ **b.** humans.
   - ☐ **c.** dinosaurs.

5. Robert Hooke discovered that plants have
   - ☐ **a.** tissues.
   - ☐ **b.** seeds.
   - ☐ **c.** cells.

Understanding Ideas

1. The topic that a botanist would be least likely to study is
   - ☐ **a.** the age of fossils.
   - ☐ **b.** the properties of electricity.
   - ☐ **c.** the breeding of fruit trees.

2. An apple tree is a
   - ☐ **a.** nonvascular plant.
   - ☐ **b.** vascular plant.
   - ☐ **c.** simple plant.

3. Plants that belong to the same phylum are
   - ☐ **a.** a rosebush and a moss.
   - ☐ **b.** a rosebush and a pine tree.
   - ☐ **c.** a rosebush and a liverwort.

4. From the article, you can conclude that
   - ☐ **a.** *phylum* is singular, and *phyla* is plural.
   - ☐ **b.** *phylum* is plural, and *phyla* is singular.
   - ☐ **c.** *phyla* refers only to nonvascular plants.

5. The most likely place to find a plant fossil is
   - ☐ **a.** on a sandy beach.
   - ☐ **b.** on the bark of a tree.
   - ☐ **c.** along the banks of a rocky stream.

C. Reading Strategies

1. Recognizing Words in Context

Find the word *identify* in the article. One definition below is closest to the meaning of that word. One definition has the opposite or nearly the opposite meaning. The remaining definition has a meaning that has nothing to do with the other two words. Label the definitions **C** for *closest*, **O** for *opposite* or *nearly opposite*, and **U** for *unrelated*.

_____ **a.** eat

_____ **b.** overlook

_____ **c.** name

2. Distinguishing Fact from Opinion

Two of the statements below present *facts*, which can be proved. The other statement is an *opinion*, which expresses someone's thoughts or beliefs. Label the statements **F** for *fact* and **O** for *opinion*.

_____ **a.** Botanist Gregor Mendel studied the characteristics of pea plants.

_____ **b.** Nonvascular plants are simpler than vascular plants.

_____ **c.** Fossils of animals are more important than fossils of plants.

3. Making Correct Inferences

Two of the statements below are correct *inferences*, or reasonable guesses, that are based on information in the article. The other statement is an incorrect, or faulty, inference. Label the statements **C** for *correct* inference and **I** for *incorrect* inference.

_____ **a.** The invention of the microscope helped botanists learn about plants.

_____ **b.** Plant phyla split plants into groups according to size.

_____ **c.** Botanists work to find new ways plants can be useful to people.

4. Understanding Main Ideas

One of the statements below expresses the main idea of the article. Another statement is too general, or too broad. The other explains only part of the article; it is too narrow. Label the statements **M** for *main idea*, **B** for *too broad*, and **N** for *too narrow*.

_____ **a.** Botanists have studied plants, their parts, and the environment for hundreds of years.

_____ **b.** Vascular plants have parts that move water and food through the plant.

_____ **c.** Botanists are scientists who study plants.

5. Responding to the Article

Complete the following sentence in your own words:

Before I read "What Is a Botanist?" I already knew

_____

_____

D. Expanding Vocabulary

Content-Area Words

Cross out one word or phrase in each row that is not related to the word in dark type.

1. taxonomy	groups	parts	botanists	food
2. characteristics	color	size	fossils	Mendel
3. bred	organize	reproduce	plants	grow
4. environment	taxonomy	health	weather	temperature
5. ecology	environment	plant	phyla	fossils

Academic English

In the article "What Is a Botanist?" you learned that *transport* is a verb that means "carry from one place to another." *Transport* can also be a noun that means "a vehicle that carries something from one place to another," as in the following sentence.

My transport from home to school is a bus.

Complete the sentence below.

1. Ships are a common *transport* across the _____

Now use the word *transport* in a sentence of your own.

2. _____

_____

You also learned that *research* is a noun that means "careful search or examination." *Research* can also be used as a verb meaning "to study or examine carefully," as in the following sentence.

I plan to research my subject well before I make my speech.

Complete the sentence below.

3. Their book shows that the authors *researched* _____

Now use the word *research* in two sentences of your own.

4. _____

5. _____

 Share your new sentences with a partner.

Lesson 3
Lakes and Rivers

Before You Read

Tip! **Think about what you know.** Read the title and the first two sentences of the article on the opposite page. Did you ever swim, fish, or ride in a boat on a lake or river?

Vocabulary

The content-area and academic English words below appear in "Lakes and Rivers." Read the definitions and the example sentences.

Content-Area Words

species (spē′shēz) a group of living things that share certain characteristics
  Example: My favorite *species* of wild cat is the tiger.

landslides (land′slīdz′) large amounts of dirt or rocks that slide down a mountain or hill
  Example: Rocks from *landslides* hit our car when we drove through the mountains.

barrier (bar′ē ər) something that separates two areas or blocks the way
  Example: The fallen tree was a *barrier* across the road, so we turned the car around and went back.

craters (krā′tərz) bowl-shaped holes in the ground around the opening of volcanoes
  Example: Smoke came from the deep *crater* around the volcano.

spring (spring) a place where water flows out of the earth
  Example: Cool, fresh water flowed from a *spring* in the ground.

Academic English

shift (shift) to change place, position, or direction
  Example: Ocean waves cause sand to *shift* on the shore.

expand (iks pand′) enlarge or increase in size
  Example: We watched the balloon *expand* as he filled it with air.

Answer the questions below. Circle the part of each question that is the answer. The first one has been done for you.

1. Do all members of a *species* (share some name), or does each have a different name?
2. Does someone's stomach *expand* when it is empty or full?
3. Would a boat go around or through a *barrier* in a river?
4. Do *landslides* bring dirt and rock down to the bottom of a mountain or up to the top of a mountain?
5. Are *craters* openings in the ground, or areas that rise above ground level?
6. If a picture hanging on the wall *shifts*, does it move or stay in place?
7. Does *spring* water fall from the sky in the spring or flow from the ground at any time?

 Now skim the article and look for other words that are new to you. Write each new word and its definition in the Personal Dictionary.

While You Read

Tip! **Think about why you read.** Have you ever heard of glacial, crater, or barrier lakes? As you read, look for information about these lakes and how they were formed.

1 Many areas of Earth are covered with water. Lakes and rivers are especially important because people and animals need them in order to live. In the United States, lakes and rivers give us 70 percent of our drinking water. They also provide homes for many **species** of animals and plants.

5 A lake is a large body, or area, of water that does not flow anywhere and is not directly connected to an ocean. Lakes are surrounded by land. Some lakes were formed after large areas of thick ice called glaciers moved over the land, scooping up and moving rocks and dirt. These lakes are called glacial lakes because they were made by glaciers. The Great Lakes are glacial lakes. Some lakes were

10 formed when **landslides** blocked areas of low land between hills or mountains, called valleys. These are called **barrier** lakes. When rain and melted snow collect in the **craters** of volcanoes, they form crater lakes, such as Green Lake in Hawaii. Tectonic lakes form in cracks in the Earth's top layer, or crust. These cracks form when large areas of rock called plates **shift** underground. Lake Tanganyika in East

15 Africa is a tectonic lake.

A river is a large body of water that flows down a hill or mountain into an ocean or a lake. A river starts at a place called a source, which can be a **spring,** a lake, or melted snow that is flowing down a mountain. The place where a river ends is called its mouth. This is where the river joins an ocean or lake. A river can

20 **expand** as it moves from its source to its mouth. It may be joined along the way by smaller rivers called streams. These rivers and streams that join a large river are called tributaries.

The source of the Mississippi River is a lake in Minnesota. The river starts as a stream so small that a person can step across it. As it flows south, it gets

25 wider because other streams and rivers join it. The Mississippi flows for about 3,200 kilometers (2,000 miles) to its mouth in the Gulf of Mexico.

A river together with its tributaries is called a river system. The entire area of land that supplies water to a river is called a drainage basin. One drainage basin is separated from another by an area of high land called a watershed, or divide.

30 Like lakes, rivers are very useful. They provide water for growing plants. Boats carrying supplies often travel on rivers. And flowing rivers can be used to make electricity.

LANGUAGE CONNECTION

A compound word is made up of two smaller words. The word *landslide* is a compound word. Find another compound word in the article or think of one on your own.

CONTENT CONNECTION

A sink is a *basin.* Water flows from the faucet into the basin and down the drain. Pipes carry it away. Outside, water flows into rivers from land known as *drainage basins.* The rivers carry the water away from the drainage basins.

After You Read

A. Organizing Ideas

What do you know or want to know about lakes and rivers? Complete the K-W-L chart below. List four things you want to learn about and four facts you have learned from the article about lakes and rivers. The first column has been done for you.

What I Know	What I Want to Know	What I Have Learned
Chicago is near Lake Michigan. Lake Michigan is one of the Great Lakes.		
Some lakes are called tectonic lakes.		
The Mississippi River is in the United States.		
Sometimes a river gets bigger as it flows toward its mouth.		

As you completed this chart, did you learn more about something you already knew about? Write two or more sentences about something new that you have learned about rivers or lakes. Will you use this type of chart again when you read something else? Why or why not?

_____

_____

_____

_____

_____

_____

B. Comprehension Skills

 Think about how to find answers. Think about what each sentence means. Try to say it to yourself in your own words before you complete it.

Mark box **a, b,** or **c** with an **X** before the choice that best completes each sentence.

Recalling Facts

1. A lake
   - ☐ **a.** flows down a slope.
   - ☐ **b.** has a source and a mouth.
   - ☐ **c.** lies in an area that is lower than the land that surrounds it.

2. A barrier lake is formed in a
   - ☐ **a.** crater of a dead volcano.
   - ☐ **b.** valley that is blocked.
   - ☐ **c.** crack in Earth's crust.

3. A river is a body of water that
   - ☐ **a.** flows down a slope into an ocean or a lake.
   - ☐ **b.** is always a result of melting snow.
   - ☐ **c.** flows for more than 1,000 kilometers (620 miles).

4. Rivers and streams that flow into a river are called
   - ☐ **a.** springs.
   - ☐ **b.** currents.
   - ☐ **c.** tributaries.

5. The percentage of drinking water in the United States that comes from lakes and rivers is
   - ☐ **a.** 25 percent.
   - ☐ **b.** 40 percent.
   - ☐ **c.** 70 percent.

Understanding Ideas

1. From the article, you can conclude that lakes are
   - ☐ **a.** sometimes formed by the movement of rock or ice.
   - ☐ **b.** wide sections of rivers.
   - ☐ **c.** always very deep.

2. A tectonic lake is probably made by
   - ☐ **a.** a thunderstorm.
   - ☐ **b.** an earthquake.
   - ☐ **c.** a watershed.

3. A river is probably widest at
   - ☐ **a.** its source.
   - ☐ **b.** a place where it is joined by a stream.
   - ☐ **c.** its mouth.

4. From the article, you can conclude that without lakes and rivers,
   - ☐ **a.** most animals would die.
   - ☐ **b.** the oceans would dry up.
   - ☐ **c.** there would be no mountains or valleys.

5. Which of the following would you probably find in a river's drainage basin?
   - ☐ **a.** a sand dune
   - ☐ **b.** a volcano
   - ☐ **c.** a swamp

C. Reading Strategies

1. Recognizing Words in Context

Find the word *supplies* in the article. One definition below is closest to the meaning of that word. One definition has the opposite or nearly the opposite meaning. The remaining definition has a meaning that has nothing to do with the other two words. Label the definitions **C** for *closest,* **O** for *opposite or nearly opposite,* and **U** for *unrelated.*

_____ **a.** gives or provides

_____ **b.** takes or uses

_____ **c.** flies or floats

2. Distinguishing Fact from Opinion

Two of the statements below present *facts,* which can be proved. The other statement is an *opinion,* which expresses someone's thoughts or beliefs. Label the statements **F** for *fact* and **O** for *opinion.*

_____ **a.** River water is more valuable than lake water.

_____ **b.** The Great Lakes were formed by large moving areas of thick ice.

_____ **c.** The source of a river provides it with water as it begins.

3. Making Correct Inferences

Two of the statements below are correct *inferences,* or reasonable guesses, that are based on information in the article. The other statement is an incorrect, or faulty, inference. Label the statements **C** for *correct* inference and **I** for *incorrect* inference.

_____ **a.** Tributaries, such as streams, add water to a river.

_____ **b.** The mouth of a river is filled with sand and dirt.

_____ **c.** Rivers are useful for transporting things from place to place.

4. Understanding Main Ideas

One of the statements below expresses the main idea of the article. Another statement is too general, or too broad. The other explains only part of the article; it is too narrow. Label the statements **M** for *main idea,* **B** for *too broad,* and **N** for *too narrow.*

_____ **a.** Rivers provide water that helps farmers grow plants.

_____ **b.** The world is covered with rivers and lakes.

_____ **c.** Lakes and rivers form in different ways and help provide the fresh water needed for life.

5. Responding to the Article

Complete the following sentence in your own words:

What interested me most in "Lakes and Rivers" was

_____

_____

D. Expanding Vocabulary

Content-Area Words

Complete each analogy with a word from the box. Write in the missing word.

| species | landslide | barrier | crater | spring |

1. avalanche : snow :: _____ : dirt and rocks

2. mountain : high :: _____ : low

3. volcano : lava :: _____ : water

4. body of water : river :: _____ : watershed

5. races : different :: _____ : similar

Academic English

In the article "Lakes and Rivers," you learned that *shift* is a verb that means "to change place, position, or direction." *Shift* can also be a noun that means "a scheduled time of work or duty," as in the following sentence.

A sailor's shift may change several times in a month.

Complete the sentence below.

1. The nurses who work on a twelve-hour *shift* are often _____

Now use the word *shift* in a sentence of your own.

2. _____

_____

You also learned that *expand* means "enlarge or increase in size." *Expand* can also mean "unfold," as in the following sentence.

You must expand the pages of a newspaper in order to read it.

Complete the sentence below.

3. This umbrella can *expand* to a diameter of _____

Now use the word *expand* in two sentences of your own.

4. _____

5. _____

 Share your new sentences with a partner.

Before You Read

 Think about what you know. Read the lesson title above. Have you ever flown on an airplane? Think about what you know about flying.

Vocabulary

The content-area and academic English words below appear in "How Flight Is Possible." Read the definitions and the example sentences.

Content-Area Words

flight (flīt) the act of flying in the air
> *Example:* We watched the bird in *flight,* and then we saw it land on the ground.

forces (fôrs′iz) forms of power or energy used on an object
> *Example:* Many *forces* pull and push on an airplane as it flies.

pressure (presh′ər) a force applied by one thing upon another
> *Example:* We all pushed hard until our *pressure* opened the heavy door.

streamlined (strēm′līnd′) having a smooth, slim shape that can move easily and quickly through air or water
> *Example:* Fish have *streamlined* bodies that help them glide easily through the water.

balance (bal′əns) a condition in which equal forces keep something steady, stable, or straight
> *Example:* She can *balance* on one foot if she holds her arms out.

Academic English

enables (i nā′bəlz) makes able or possible
> *Example:* The wind *enables* a kite to fly.

alter (ôl′tər) change or make different
> *Example:* I will *alter* the dress to make it fit better.

Rate each vocabulary word according to the following scale. Write a number next to each content-area and academic English word.

<u>4</u> I have never seen the word before.

<u>3</u> I have seen the word but do not know what it means.

<u>2</u> I know what the word means when I read it.

<u>1</u> I use the word myself in speaking or writing.

 Now skim the article and look for other words that are new to you. Write each new word and its definition in the Personal Dictionary.

While You Read

Tip! **Think about why you read.** How do you think birds and airplanes fly? Write a question about flying that you would like to know the answer to. As you read, you may find the answer.

How Flight Is Possible

1   A jet plane moves down an airport runway, gaining speed until it lifts off the ground. A bird flaps its wings and flies off into the sky. Once in **flight,** both the plane and the bird fly smoothly through the air. What **enables** each one to be able to leave the ground, or take off, and stay up in the air?

5   The answer is partly because of the shapes and features of their bodies. The body of a bird is covered with feathers. Its body is also very light because many of its bones are empty inside, or hollow. The shape of its wings and its smooth, thin body are perfect for flight. Like birds, airplanes have smooth, slim bodies with wings. Unlike birds, planes have engines that allow them to lift off the

10 ground and stay in flight. Flight is possible for both birds and planes because they are able to work with four **forces** involved in flight. These forces are lift, thrust, drag, and gravity.

        Lift occurs as the wings of a bird or a plane move through air. Both kinds of wings are curved on top and flat on the bottom. Air flows more quickly over the

15 curved top than it does over the flat bottom. This reduces the air **pressure** on the top of the wing, which pulls the bird or plane up.

        Birds and planes need thrust to make air flow over the wings to create lift. Thrust is the force that moves a bird or plane forward. To create thrust, a bird flaps its wings, and a plane uses one or more engines.

20   Drag is caused by air flowing against the body of the plane or the bird. Drag is a force that pushes against an object and slows it down. We describe the smooth, slim bodies of birds and planes as **streamlined.** The form of their bodies helps reduce drag so they can go fast enough to lift off the ground.

        Gravity, or the downward pull of Earth, is the force that both planes and birds

25 must work against to get off the ground. Because a plane is heavy, it needs a lot of thrust to produce enough lift to work against gravity so that it can take off. In the air, the shape of the bird or plane creates **balance.** That is the reason gravity does not cause it to dive downward or to swing from side to side. The tails of birds and planes help them stay balanced. Birds and planes can **alter** direction by moving

30 their wings and tails just a little bit. They also must make changes to deal with different wind speeds and directions.

LANGUAGE CONNECTION

The phrase *take off* means *remove.* For example: *Take off your shoes. Take off* also means *leave the ground.* For example: *The plane will take off when the pilot is ready.* Can you use the phrase *take off,* in this sense, in a sentence of your own?

CONTENT CONNECTION

Birds are not the only living things that have streamlined bodies. So do water animals. River otters have short, waterproof fur and small ears that lie flat and help them swim. Can you think of other living or nonliving things that have streamlined shapes?

After You Read

A. Organizing Ideas

What are the four forces of flight? Complete the chart below. Write down the names of the forces of flight on the lines above the boxes. In each box, write two sentences that explain the force named. Refer to the article to help you. The first box has been done for you.

The Forces of Flight

Lift _____

> As birds and planes fly, their wings create lift. Air flows more quickly over the curved tops of the wings. That reduces air pressure on the tops of the wings, which pulls the bird or the plane upward.

_____

_____

_____

How did this chart help you understand the forces of flight? Write two or more sentences about how well you understand the four forces.

_____

_____

_____

_____

_____

_____

_____

B. Comprehension Skills

 Think about how to find answers. Look back at different parts of the text. What facts help you figure out how to complete the sentences?

Mark box **a, b,** or **c** with an **X** before the choice that best completes each sentence.

Recalling Facts

1. Birds' bodies are lightweight partly because they have many
   - ☐ **a.** small organs.
   - ☐ **b.** hollow bones.
   - ☐ **c.** feathery wings.

2. Lift, thrust, drag, and gravity are
   - ☐ **a.** forces that are part of flight.
   - ☐ **b.** built into jets today.
   - ☐ **c.** types of air pressure.

3. The force that pulls birds and planes up as air flows past wings is
   - ☐ **a.** gravity.
   - ☐ **b.** magnetism.
   - ☐ **c.** lift.

4. The flapping wings of a bird and the engine of a plane both produce
   - ☐ **a.** thrust.
   - ☐ **b.** drag.
   - ☐ **c.** gravity.

5. The tops of the wings on birds and planes are
   - ☐ **a.** flat.
   - ☐ **b.** curved.
   - ☐ **c.** bumpy.

Understanding Ideas

1. You can assume that a streamlined body is
   - ☐ **a.** smooth and sleek.
   - ☐ **b.** full of energy.
   - ☐ **c.** connected to wings and feet.

2. From the article, you can conclude that a bird or a plane without a tail would find it hard to
   - ☐ **a.** take off.
   - ☐ **b.** overcome gravity.
   - ☐ **c.** change directions.

3. Although a bird can simply flap its wings for thrust, a plane needs an engine because
   - ☐ **a.** it has long wings.
   - ☐ **b.** it is not lightweight.
   - ☐ **c.** it has narrow wings.

4. From the article, you can conclude that the largest airplanes need
   - ☐ **a.** very thick wings.
   - ☐ **b.** as few passengers as possible.
   - ☐ **c.** very powerful engines.

5. The author suggests that flight is possible mostly because of
   - ☐ **a.** four forces.
   - ☐ **b.** thrust and body shape.
   - ☐ **c.** powerful wings and jet engines.

C. Reading Strategies

1. Recognizing Words in Context

Find the word *reduce* in the article. One definition below is closest to the meaning of that word. One definition has the opposite or nearly the opposite meaning. The remaining definition has a meaning that has nothing to do with the other two words. Label the definitions **C** for *closest,* **O** for *opposite* or *nearly opposite,* and **U** for *unrelated.*

_____ **a.** decrease, or make less

_____ **b.** halt, or stop completely

_____ **c.** increase, or make more

2. Distinguishing Fact from Opinion

Two of the statements below present *facts,* which can be proved. The other statement is an *opinion,* which expresses someone's thoughts or beliefs. Label the statements **F** for *fact* and **O** for *opinion.*

_____ **a.** Air flows more quickly and easily over curved objects than over flat ones.

_____ **b.** If the force of drag is increased, an airplane will move more slowly.

_____ **c.** If airplanes were covered with feathers, they might fly faster.

3. Making Correct Inferences

Two of the statements below are correct *inferences,* or reasonable guesses, that are based on information in the article. The other statement is an incorrect, or faulty, inference. Label the statements **C** for *correct* inference and **I** for *incorrect* inference.

_____ **a.** If air pressure above a bird's wing increases, the bird will fly higher and faster.

_____ **b.** Tails help birds and airplanes balance and change directions.

_____ **c.** Thrust moves a bird or plane forward.

4. Understanding Main Ideas

One of the statements below expresses the main idea of the article. Another statement is too general, or too broad. The other explains only part of the article; it is too narrow. Label the statements **M** for *main idea,* **B** for *too broad,* and **N** for *too narrow.*

_____ **a.** Birds and airplanes fly because of their shapes and because of the forces of lift, thrust, drag, and gravity.

_____ **b.** Flying is an easy way for birds and airplanes to move through the air.

_____ **c.** Planes' engines help them lift off the ground and fly through the air.

5. Responding to the Article

Complete the following sentence in your own words:
One thing in "How Flight Is Possible" that I cannot understand is

_____

_____

D. Expanding Vocabulary

Content-Area Words

Complete each sentence with a word from the box. Write the missing word on the line.

| forces | pressure | flight | balance | streamlined |

1. Birds and planes can stay in the air because their bodies are designed for _____.

2. The wings of birds and planes are shaped so that air _____ above the wings is reduced.

3. _____ such as drag and gravity make a bird work to stay in the air.

4. A submarine and a rocket both have sleek, _____ bodies.

5. Birds use their tails to keep their _____ while they fly.

Academic English

In the article "How Flight Is Possible," you learned that *enables* means "makes able or possible." *Enables* can relate to making flight possible. *Enables* can also relate to making other things possible, as in the following sentence.

Your nose enables you to recognize different smells.

Complete the sentence below.

1. A microwave oven *enables* people to_____

Now use the word *enables* in a sentence of your own.

2. _____

_____

You also learned that *alter* means "change or make different." *Alter* can relate to how a bird changes directions in flight. *Alter* can also relate to other things that change or become different, as in the following sentence.

Music can alter the way people feel.

Complete the sentence below.

3. He *alters* the taste of foods by using seasonings such as_____

Now use the word *alter* in two sentences of your own.

4. _____

5. _____

 Share your new sentences with a partner.

Before You Read

Tip! **Think what you know.** Read the first two sentences of the article on the opposite page. What do you think the article might be about? Did you know that Earth has layers?

Vocabulary

The content-area and academic English words below appear in "Earth's Layers." Read the definitions and the example sentences.

Content-Area Words

mantle (man′təl) the part of Earth that surrounds the central core
    Example: The thickest part of our planet is its *mantle.*

continental (kon′tə nent′əl) relating to the landmasses of the seven continents, or large areas of land on Earth
    Example: We must stay in the *continental* United States, so we will not fly to Hawaii.

minerals (min′ər əlz) things—such as gold, coal, or water—that are made by nature and are usually found in the ground
    Example: Some people work underground to dig for *minerals* such as coal and gold.

average (av′rij) the sum of a set of values divided by the number of values
    Example: The *average* number of students in each class is 23.

solar system (sō′lər sis′təm) the Sun and every heavenly body that circles it
    Example: If you build a model of the *solar system,* start with the Sun at the center.

Academic English

core (kôr) the center part
    Example: The seeds of an apple are in its *core.*

consists (kən sists′) is made (of)
    Example: My favorite sandwich *consists* of bread, peanut butter, and honey.

Complete the sentences below that contain the content-area and academic English words above. Use the spaces provided. The first one has been done for you.

1. Our *solar system* includes <u>the Sun and everything that circles it</u>.
2. We learned that gold is a *mineral* because it is found _____.
3. Earth's *mantle* surrounds _____.
4. Earth's *core* is found in _____.
5. The *average* temperature in June is _____.
6. You can tell what a can of food *consists* of by reading _____.
7. The *continental* United States is made up of _____.

 Now skim the article and look for other words that are new to you. Write each new word and its definition in the Personal Dictionary.

While You Read

 Think about why you read. The top layer of our planet is called the crust. As you read, try to find out how thick the crust is.

Earth's
Layers

1 The planet Earth is made of four layers: the crust, the **mantle,** the outer **core,** and the inner core. Earth is changing all the time because of the high pressures and temperatures deep inside it.

The surface, or crust, of Earth **consists** of rocky sections, called plates, that 5 move very slowly. Land is made of the **continental** crust, which is mainly very hard rock called granite. Most of this crust formed when hot, liquid rock called magma rose from below Earth's surface and hardened. The oceanic crust is found under the oceans. It is made up mostly of the **minerals** silicon oxide and magnesium oxide. These minerals come mostly from volcanoes. Earth's crust has 10 an **average** thickness of about 10 kilometers (6 miles) under the oceans. Under the continents, the average thickness is about 40 kilometers (25 miles). The crust is a thin layer compared to the layers below it.

Unlike the crust, which is hard and thin, the mantle is soft and thick. It is made of very hot rock that flows slowly, like thick mud. This hot rock contains a great 15 deal of the metal called iron. The mantle is about 2,900 kilometers (1,800 miles) thick and is Earth's thickest layer. The part of the mantle that is closer to the center of Earth is hotter than the part that is farther away from the center. Many scientists believe that the material rises when it is at its hottest and then sinks as it cools. Movement of the liquid rock in the mantle causes the crust above it to 20 move. This movement is called an earthquake.

The mantle is found around Earth's outer, or outside, core. The outer core is so much hotter than the mantle that the metals found there are liquid. They consist mostly of iron and nickel. The outer core is about 2,300 kilometers (1,400 miles) thick. Beneath it is the inner core, which is the center of Earth. This round area 25 is about 2,575 kilometers (1,600 miles) across. It is the hottest and heaviest layer of all. Like the outer core, it is made up mostly of iron and nickel. Unlike the metal in the outer core, the metal in the inner core is solid because of the high pressure there.

Scientists believe that when Earth was a young planet, it crashed into many 30 other objects while the **solar system** was forming. This made Earth very hot. As it cooled, the heaviest material sank to the center and stayed hot. The lightest material moved outward to form the crust.

CONTENT CONNECTION

Earth has four layers. A cut orange has layers of peel, fruit, and seeds. A road has layers of tar, gravel, and other materials. Describe the layers in the walls of a house, a watermelon, or a coat.

LANGUAGE CONNECTION

A suffix is a group of letters added to a word. Knowing the meaning of a suffix helps us understand the meaning of that word. The suffix -*est* means "most," so *brightest* means "the most bright." Can you find three words in the article that end with the suffix -*est*?

After You Read

A. Organizing Ideas

What are Earth's four layers? Complete the circle chart below to arrange this information. Write down the name of each of Earth's layers. Under each name, write three facts about that layer. The first one has been done for you.

The Layers of Earth

Crust _____

1. Earth's rocky surface is called the crust. _____

2. Its average thickness under the oceans is 10 kilometers (6 miles). _____

3. The crust is made of large pieces, called plates, that move slowly. _____

_____

1. _____

2. _____

3. _____

_____

1. _____

2. _____

3. _____

_____

1. _____

2. _____

3. _____

How did this chart help you understand the layers of Earth?
Write two or more sentences to compare or contrast two of the layers.

_____

_____

_____

_____

B. Comprehension Skills

 Think about how to find answers. Look back at what you read. The information is in the text, but you may have to look in several sentences to find it.

Mark box **a, b,** or **c** with an **X** before the choice that best completes each sentence.

Recalling Facts

1. The oceanic crust
   - ☐ **a.** is found only under the ocean.
   - ☐ **b.** is part of Earth's mantle.
   - ☐ **c.** is under the ocean and the continents.

2. Earth's crust is
   - ☐ **a.** soft and thin.
   - ☐ **b.** soft and thick.
   - ☐ **c.** hard and thin.

3. The mantle consists of
   - ☐ **a.** solid metals
   - ☐ **b.** liquid metals.
   - ☐ **c.** very hot rock that flows like hot tar.

4. Earth's thickest layer is
   - ☐ **a.** the crust.
   - ☐ **b.** the mantle.
   - ☐ **c.** the outer core.

5. As the young planet Earth cooled, the heaviest material
   - ☐ **a.** sank to the center.
   - ☐ **b.** rose to the top.
   - ☐ **c.** formed the mantle.

Understanding Ideas

1. We can easily imagine how Earth's layers look by comparing them to the layers of a
   - ☐ **a.** round rock.
   - ☐ **b.** peach half that shows the skin, flesh, and pit.
   - ☐ **c.** slice of frosted cake.

2. From the article, you can conclude that
   - ☐ **a.** each layer of Earth is the same temperature.
   - ☐ **b.** the deeper the layer, the cooler the temperature.
   - ☐ **c.** the deeper the layer, the hotter the temperature.

3. It is most likely that the high pressure in the inner core comes from
   - ☐ **a.** the weight of the layers above the inner core.
   - ☐ **b.** gases deep inside Earth.
   - ☐ **c.** high temperatures.

4. From the article, you can conclude that
   - ☐ **a.** iron will melt only at a very high temperature.
   - ☐ **b.** Earth consists of iron and things that contain iron.
   - ☐ **c.** all layers of Earth are divided into plates.

5. You can also conclude that earthquakes are probably caused by
   - ☐ **a.** the movements of plates.
   - ☐ **b.** large ocean waves.
   - ☐ **c.** the solid iron in the inner core.

C. Reading Strategies

1. Recognizing Words in Context

Find the word *surface* in the article. One definition below is closest to the meaning of that word. One definition has the opposite or nearly the opposite meaning. The remaining definition has a meaning that has nothing to do with the other two words. Label the definitions **C** for *closest,* **O** for *opposite* or *nearly opposite,* and **U** for *unrelated.*

_____ **a.** covering

_____ **b.** mountains

_____ **c.** inside

2. Distinguishing Fact from Opinion

Two of the statements below present *facts,* which can be proved. The other statement is an *opinion,* which expresses someone's thoughts or beliefs. Label the statements **F** for *fact* and **O** for *opinion.*

_____ **a.** The oceans rest on top of the oceanic crust.

_____ **b.** The mineral silicon oxide is shiny and beautiful.

_____ **c.** The inner core is the hottest and heaviest layer of Earth.

3. Making Correct Inferences

Two of the statements below are correct *inferences,* or reasonable guesses, that are based on information in the article. The other statement is an incorrect, or faulty, inference. Label the statements **C** for *correct* inference and **I** for *incorrect* inference.

_____ **a.** We can see Earth's crust move whenever liquid rock in the mantle moves.

_____ **b.** The outer core is so hot that the metal found there is liquid.

_____ **c.** The part of the mantle that is close to Earth's core is hotter than the part that is farther away from it.

4. Understanding Main Ideas

One of the statements below expresses the main idea of the article. Another statement is too general, or too broad. The other explains only part of the article; it is too narrow. Label the statements **M** for *main idea,* **B** for *too broad,* and **N** for *too narrow.*

_____ **a.** The outer core surrounding the inner core consists of hot, liquid iron and nickel.

_____ **b.** Earth's four layers—crust, mantle, outer core, and inner core—get hotter as they get closer to Earth's center.

_____ **c.** Earth changes all the time because it has many temperatures and types of pressure inside of it.

5. Responding to the Article

Complete the following sentence in your own words:

From reading "Earth's Layers," I have learned _____

_____

D. Expanding Vocabulary

Content-Area Words

Read each item carefully. Write on the line the word or phrase that best completes each sentence.

1. The pressure is highest in Earth's _____.
   mantle   inner core   outer core   crust

2. Continental crust, consisting mostly of _____, is the land that we live on.
   granite   minerals   volcanoes   thick mud

3. The oceanic crust is made of minerals that come mostly from _____.
   planets   the Sun   the stars   volcanoes

4. The metal in Earth's inner core is solid because of the great _____ on it.
   pressure   crust   heat   air

5. The planets and _____ make up the solar system.
   magma   the Sun   the core   minerals

Academic English

In the article "Earth's Layers," you learned that *core* can be a noun that means "the center part." *Core* can also be a verb that means "to remove the core of," as in the following sentence.

   Please cut these pears in half and then core them.

Complete the sentence below.

1. Are you able to *core* an apple without _____

Now use the word *core* in a sentence of your own.

2. _____

You also learned that *consists* means "is made (of)." *Consists* can describe what makes up Earth's crust. *Consist* can also mean "have a basis (in)," as in the following sentence.

   A good life consists in leaving the world better than you found it.

Complete the sentence below.

3. Wisdom *consists* in _____

Now use the word *consists* in two sentences of your own.

4. _____

5. _____

 Share your new sentences with a partner.

Reading a Newspaper Article

Read the newspaper article. Then complete the sentences.
Use words from the Word Bank.

Word Bank

enables   goal
alter   species
environment

Daily News • Science

Environmental Group Concerned About Rare Plant

A group of citizens talked about a rare plant _____ at a city meeting Tuesday night. The members of Friends of the _____ said that they are worried about a new gas station that someone is planning to build near the state park. Putting a building so close to the park will _____ the habitat of the plant, they said. "Our _____ is to protect the Purple Sunset iris," said Delia Ortiz, a member. "The new building may disrupt growing conditions. The location _____ the Purple Sunset iris to survive here." The group wants the city to lead the community in protecting the plant. The city is considering the request.

Writing a Journal

Read the entry from the journal of astronaut Sasha Lim. Circle the word that completes each sentence.

March 14

Our space (**flight, core**) has continued without any major problems. I spent most of the morning doing (**craters, calculations**) so that we could figure out how much fuel and oxygen are left on the spaceship. I have used my own camera to take pictures of a satellite as it (**orbits, transports**) Earth. It will be fun to show the pictures to my family when I get home. Tomorrow we will be landing on the Moon. I have read so much about its deep (**craters, research**) that I am eager to see the surface myself. We will collect samples of the Moon's rocky surface and (**orbit, transport**) them back to Earth.

 **Making Connections**

Work with a partner. Talk about what the words mean. How can you use the words to talk about an airplane? List your ideas in the outline of the airplane below.

altitudes	**rocket**	**consists**	**pressure**	**streamlined**
balance	**shift**	**expand**	**cooperated**	**ecology**

Use all of the words above in complete sentences of your own. Each sentence may include one or more of the words. To help you start writing, look at the ideas you wrote about. After you write your sentences, read them over. If you find a mistake, correct it.

_____

_____

_____

_____

_____

_____

_____

_____

Before You Read

 Think about what you know. Read the title and the first two sentences of the article on the opposite page. Have you ever heard of the Nobel Prizes?

Vocabulary

The content-area and academic English words below appear in "The Nobel Prizes." Read the definitions and the example sentences.

Content-Area Words

dynamite (dī'nə mīt') an explosive, or substance that bursts into flame easily, made with a chemical called nitroglycerin

> *Example:* The old, empty building fell after the *dynamite* exploded.

will (wil) an official paper that states what should happen to a person's money or possessions after he or she dies

> *Example:* In her *will,* she directed that her house and her money be given to her children.

fund (fund) money set aside and ready for a specific purpose

> *Example:* I used money from my transportation *fund* to pay to have my car repaired.

document (dok'yə mənt) something written that gives important information

> *Example:* This *document* proves that I am a citizen.

honors (on'ərz) special credits or symbols of great respect given to people who deserve or have earned them

> *Example:* The president gave the soldier special *honors* for her bravery.

Academic English

establish (es tab'lish) to build or set up

> *Example:* We will *establish* a place where students can meet and play sports after school.

author (ô'thər) one who writes a book or other type of literature

> *Example:* That *author* wrote my favorite book about baseball.

Answer the questions below. Circle the part of each question that is the answer. The first one has been done for you.

1. If you *establish* a bank account, do you (begin using it) or stop using it?
2. Do people receive *honors* by buying them or by earning them?
3. Is *dynamite* used to build things or to destroy things?
4. Is money in a *fund* used for a specific purpose or for any purpose at all?
5. Would *authors* write or sing?
6. Do you listen to or read a *document?*
7. Does Mrs. Rashid's *will* state who will own her house after she dies or while she is alive?

 Now skim the article and look for other words that are new to you. Write each new word and its definition in the Personal Dictionary.

While You Read

Tip! **Think about why you read.** Have you ever won a prize, honor, or award? The Nobel Prizes are famous awards given to people for many different reasons. As you read, try to find those reasons.

The Nobel Prizes

1 The famous awards known as the Nobel Prizes are named after a man named Alfred Nobel. Nobel was a chemist from Sweden who invented **dynamite.** He also invented other things, and he built factories around the world. He became very rich. He was interested in peace, or the idea that people should live without
5 war and fighting. Nobel also wrote poems.

Alfred Nobel died in 1896. In his **will,** he left almost nine million dollars to **establish** a **fund** to award prizes. The prizes were to be given out once a year to people who had done a great job helping others.

The will stated that there should be five different types of prizes. One prize
10 would be for the most important new idea in physics. Physics is the science that studies the relationship between objects and energy. Another prize would be for chemistry. Chemistry is the science that studies what things are made of and the changes that they go through. The third prize would be for important work in medicine. The fourth prize would be in literature, to be given to an **author** who
15 wrote an important book. The fifth prize would go to a person who worked to help spread peace around the world. In his will, Nobel said that the judges who picked the winners should not care about where a person lived.

The first Nobel Prizes were awarded in 1901. In addition to money, each prizewinner received a medal and a diploma. The diploma is a very special
20 **document** that **honors** the person who has earned the prize. In 1968 the Bank of Sweden gave money to add a prize in economics. Economics is the study of how goods and services are bought and sold.

No more than three people can share a prize unless all of them belong to the same group working for peace. Sometimes two people win a prize. Other times
25 just one person does. There have been years when one of the different prizes has not been given out. Since 1950 only the Nobel Prize in peace (and the one in economics, because it did not exist until 1968) has not been won every year.

Probably the most famous scientist to win a Nobel Prize was Albert Einstein. He was awarded the Nobel Prize in physics in 1921. Einstein received his award
30 because he used physics and mathematics in new and amazing ways to study light. Some scientists have won more than one Nobel Prize. Linus Pauling won Nobel Prizes in both chemistry and peace. Marie Curie won prizes in both physics and chemistry. A Nobel Prize is considered one of the world's highest honors.

LANGUAGE CONNECTION

Someone who is "named after" another person has the same name as that person. For example, a child who is named after his grandfather has the same name as his grandfather. Some cultures do not permit parents to name a child after someone who is still living. Do you know anyone who is named after someone else?

CONTENT CONNECTION

Many people—doctors, writers, and teachers— assist groups called the Nobel Committees. The committees study the work of each prize *candidate*, or person who hopes to win the prize. How do you think the committees recommend possible winners?

After You Read

A. Organizing Ideas

What do you know about the Nobel Prizes? Complete the outline below for the article. Write the headings or facts about the prizes on the lines. Refer to the article to find information. Some parts have been done for you.

The Nobel Prizes

I. Who was Alfred Nobel?
   - A. Swedish chemist and inventor
   - B. _____
   - C. Believer in world peace
   - D. Poet

II. What did Nobel leave to the world?
   - A. His inventions and his goals
   - B. _____
     1. _____
     2. To help continue work that helps others

III. What kinds of help to the world do the Nobel Prizes recognize?
   - A. _____
     1. Physics is the science that deals with objects and energy.
     2. _____
   - B. Chemistry
     1. _____
        _____
     2. Linus Pauling and Marie Curie both won Nobel Prizes in chemistry.
   - C. _____
   - D. Literature
   - E. _____
     1. _____
     2. Linus Pauling won prizes for spreading peace and for chemistry.
   - F. Economics
     1. _____
     2. In 1968 the Bank of Sweden gave money to add this prize to the five others.

IV. _____
   - A. Sharing a prize
   - B. _____

What have you learned from the facts in your outline? Write two or more sentences about one of the Nobel Prizes that you wrote about in your outline. Did the outline help you organize the facts in a clear way? Explain your answer.

_____

_____

B. Comprehension Skills

 Think about how to find answers. Think about what each sentence means. Try to say it to yourself in your own words before you complete it.

Mark box **a, b,** or **c** with an **X** before the choice that best completes each sentence.

Recalling Facts

1. Alfred Nobel
   - ☐ **a.** invented dynamite.
   - ☐ **b.** won the first Nobel Prize.
   - ☐ **c.** did important work in mathematics.

2. Alfred Nobel's will established that there must be
   - ☐ **a.** prizewinners who live only in Europe.
   - ☐ **b.** a prize for the study of plants.
   - ☐ **c.** five prizes.

3. The Bank of Sweden established a Nobel Prize in
   - ☐ **a.** economics.
   - ☐ **b.** mathematics.
   - ☐ **c.** history.

4. Today a Nobel Prize in any category but one can be given to
   - ☐ **a.** only one person.
   - ☐ **b.** no more than three people.
   - ☐ **c.** any number of people.

5. People who have won two Nobel Prizes include
   - ☐ **a.** Albert Einstein and Linus Pauling.
   - ☐ **b.** Albert Einstein and Marie Curie.
   - ☐ **c.** Linus Pauling and Marie Curie.

Understanding Ideas

1. From the article, you can conclude that one of Nobel's goals was to
   - ☐ **a.** help build weapons to help countries defend themselves.
   - ☐ **b.** help make the world a better place.
   - ☐ **c.** give all of his money to scientists.

2. Someone in a field in which no Nobel Prize is given is
   - ☐ **a.** a novelist.
   - ☐ **b.** a doctor.
   - ☐ **c.** an actor.

3. From the article, you can conclude that a person who has won a Nobel Prize
   - ☐ **a.** is a scientist.
   - ☐ **b.** is creative and curious.
   - ☐ **c.** has made a great discovery.

4. You can also conclude that when Nobel Prizes are not awarded, the reason is that
   - ☐ **a.** not enough important work was done in some category that year.
   - ☐ **b.** no one wanted an award.
   - ☐ **c.** there was not enough money to give to a winner.

5. You can also conclude that Nobel probably thought that
   - ☐ **a.** literature was more important than medicine.
   - ☐ **b.** the most important discoveries were in physics.
   - ☐ **c.** there are many ways for people to help other people.

C. Reading Strategies

1. Recognizing Words in Context

Find the word *considered* in the article. One definition below is closest to the meaning of that word. One definition has the opposite or nearly the opposite meaning. The remaining definition has a meaning that has nothing to do with the other two words. Label the definitions **C** for *closest*, **O** for *opposite* or *nearly opposite*, and **U** for *unrelated*.

_____ **a.** ignored

_____ **b.** thought to be

_____ **c.** inside

2. Distinguishing Fact from Opinion

Two of the statements below present *facts*, which can be proved. The other statement is an *opinion*, which expresses someone's thoughts or beliefs. Label the statements **F** for *fact* and **O** for *opinion*.

_____ **a.** Nobel Prize winners are given money, a medal, and a diploma.

_____ **b.** More than three people working together can share a Nobel Prize.

_____ **c.** Albert Einstein should have won a Nobel Prize in literature.

3. Making Correct Inferences

Two of the statements below are correct *inferences*, or reasonable guesses, that are based on information in the article. The other statement is an incorrect inference. Label the statements **C** for *correct* inference and **I** for *incorrect* inference.

_____ **a.** A Nobel Prize is given to someone who has worked very hard in one of six areas.

_____ **b.** Someone who wins a Nobel Prize can feel very proud of that honor.

_____ **c.** Alfred Nobel believed that science was more important than literature.

4. Understanding Main Ideas

One of the statements below expresses the main idea of the article. Another statement is too general, or too broad. The other explains only part of the article; it is too narrow. Label the statements **M** for *main idea*, **B** for *too broad*, and **N** for *too narrow*.

_____ **a.** Alfred Nobel created Nobel Prizes so that people who helped others could be rewarded for their good work.

_____ **b.** People who do a great job helping others should be rewarded.

_____ **c.** Since 1950 only the Nobel Prizes for peace and for economics have not been won every year.

5. Responding to the Article

Complete the following sentence in your own words:

Before I read "The Nobel Prizes," I thought

_____ ,

but now I know _____

D. Expanding Vocabulary

Content-Area Words

Cross out one word or phrase in each row that is not related to the word in dark type.

1. dynamite	explode	hot	flight	fire
2. will	official	volunteer	paper	after death
3. fund	physics	money	Alfred Nobel	population
4. document	paper	information	war	important
5. honors	award	special	Nobel Prize	voice

Academic English

In the article "The Nobel Prizes," you learned that *establish* means "to build or set up." *Establish* can refer to how Alfred Nobel set up funds for his prizes. *Establish* can also mean "to cause to grow and multiply," as in the following sentence.

How did your father establish such a good lawn in sandy soil?

Complete the sentence below.

1. He was able to *establish* a publishing house that soon _____

Now use the word *establish* in a sentence of your own.

2. _____

_____

You also learned that *author* means "one who writes a book or other type of literature." *Author* can also be a verb that means "to write text or literature," as in the following sentence.

Reporters often author articles in newspapers.

Complete the sentence below.

3. People can *author* articles for magazines as well as _____

Now use the word *author* in two sentences of your own.

4. _____

5. _____

 Share your new sentences with a partner.

Before You Read

Tip! **Think about what you know.** Read the lesson title above. Can you name one of the organs in your body?

Vocabulary

The content-area and academic English words below appear in "The Organs of the Body." Read the definitions and the example sentences.

Content-Area Words

cells (selz) the simplest units of all living things: people, animals, and plants
> *Example:* My body, my cat's body, and my tomato plant are all made of millions of *cells*.

tissues (tish′o͞oz) groups of cells that are alike and doing the same job
> *Example:* Your muscles are made of different *tissues* that work together.

oxygen (ok′sə jən) colorless, odorless gas in the air that people and animals breathe in
> *Example:* Divers breathe in *oxygen* from tanks when they are underwater.

carbon dioxide (kär′bən dī ok′sīd) colorless, odorless gas that people and animals breathe out
> *Example:* As she blew into the balloon, she exhaled *carbon dioxide* gas.

intestine (in tes′tin) an area like a tube inside the body where food is broken down
> *Example:* Food moves from the stomach to the small *intestine* to be used by the body.

Academic English

distributes (dis trib′ūts) divides (something) among people or things
> *Example:* The teacher will *distribute* books to all of the students.

transforms (trans fôrmz′) changes the way something looks, behaves, or is built
> *Example:* Bakers *transform* the sugar, flour, yeast, and water into bread.

Do any of the words above seem related? Sort the seven vocabulary words into two or more categories. Write the words down on note cards or in a chart. Words may fit into more than one group. You may wish to work with a partner for this activity. Label one category *In the Body*.

Now skim the article and look for other words that are new to you. Write each new word and its definition in the Personal Dictionary.

While You Read

Tip! **Think about why you read.** The heart, blood, and lungs work together in the body. As you read, look for information that tells you what these organs do.

THE ORGANS OF THE BODY

1   The human body is an amazing machine. Inside it are billions of tiny units called **cells.** They do the jobs that keep people alive. The body is working every second of the day. Even while a person is sleeping, the body breathes and pumps blood to all of its parts. Most people do not understand how the body works, and scientists are only beginning to understand it.

5   The billions of cells inside the body are grouped into **tissues.** Each tissue has a job. For example, there are tissues inside your mouth and tissues that make up your muscles. Even your heart is made up of tissues. The heart is one example of a group of tissues called an organ.

An organ is just a group of two or more kinds of tissue that has one important
10 job. The heart's job is to pump blood throughout the body. All of the tissues in the heart work to pump blood. The heart is known as a vital organ because it is so important that the body cannot live without it. As the heart pumps, it moves blood and **distributes oxygen** to all of the tissues. All other organs need the heart because they need oxygen to survive. The body also needs other organs. However,
15 the brain and the heart are probably the most important organs of all.

Organs that work together are called organ systems. One example of an organ system is the circulatory system. This system includes the heart, the blood, and the lungs. The job of the circulatory system is to circulate blood, or move it around the body. The lungs help this system by putting oxygen into the blood and taking
20 **carbon dioxide** out of it. When the heart pumps blood into the lungs, the blood picks up oxygen and carries it to other tissues.

Another example of an organ system is the digestive system, which is the system in the body that processes the food that people eat. This system **transforms** food into the energy that cells need to do their work. The digestive
25 system begins with two organs: the tongue and the esophagus. Food enters the body through the mouth. After the food is chewed, the tongue moves it into the esophagus. The esophagus is a long tube that moves the food from the mouth into the stomach, another organ. Food is stored in the stomach until it is mixed with a digestive liquid, which breaks it up into smaller pieces. The food then moves
30 to the small **intestine,** where it is mixed with other liquids. Any food that is not digested moves into the large intestine.

LANGUAGE CONNECTION

A *scientist* is an expert in science. Scientists study topics such as the human body or chemical reactions. They share information and ideas so that other people can learn. If you were a scientist, what would you like to study?

CONTENT CONNECTION

An *organ system* involves several organs that work together. Think about other systems. For example, buying groceries might require a system too. What people might be the "organs" that make the shopping activity work?

After You Read

A. Organizing Ideas

How does food move through your digestive system? Complete the sequence chain below. Inside each circle, write the name of an organ. Then write one or two sentences about what each organ does. Use information from the article. One circle has been done for you.

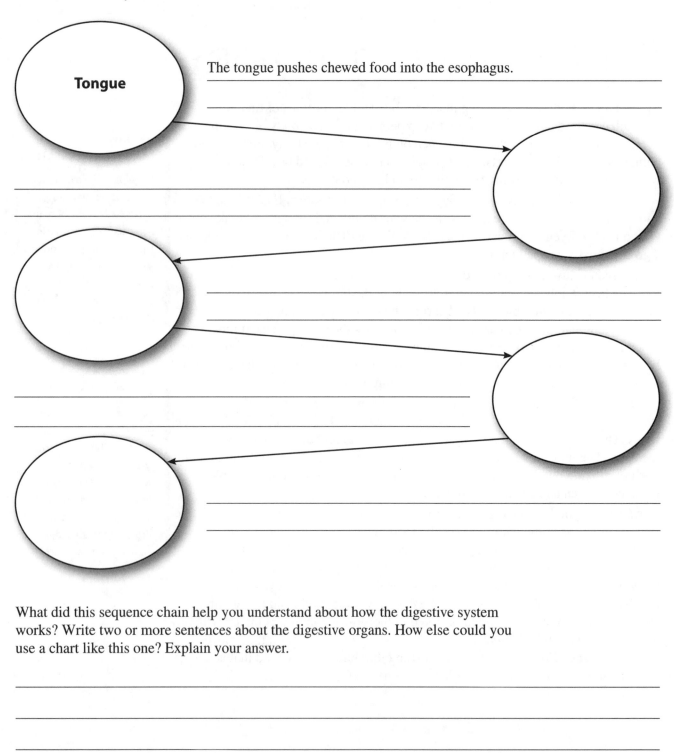

Tongue

The tongue pushes chewed food into the esophagus.

What did this sequence chain help you understand about how the digestive system works? Write two or more sentences about the digestive organs. How else could you use a chart like this one? Explain your answer.

_____

_____

_____

B. Comprehension Skills

 Think about how to find answers. Think about what each sentence means. Try to say it to yourself in your own words before you complete it.

Mark box **a, b,** or **c** with an **X** before the choice that best completes each sentence.

Recalling Facts

1. The body is made of billions of tiny units called
   - ☐ **a.** organs.
   - ☐ **b.** cells.
   - ☐ **c.** systems.

2. A group of cells that work together to do a job is called a
   - ☐ **a.** tissue.
   - ☐ **b.** molecule.
   - ☐ **c.** bloodstream.

3. The digestive system is an example of
   - ☐ **a.** an organ.
   - ☐ **b.** an organ system.
   - ☐ **c.** a tissue.

4. The long tube that moves food from the mouth to the stomach is called the
   - ☐ **a.** heart.
   - ☐ **b.** large intestine.
   - ☐ **c.** esophagus.

5. An organ is made up of at least
   - ☐ **a.** two or more types of tissue.
   - ☐ **b.** three or more types of tissue.
   - ☐ **c.** one type of tissue.

Understanding Ideas

1. While people sleep, they breathe and their hearts beat; therefore,
   - ☐ **a.** most parts of the brain are wide awake at night.
   - ☐ **b.** some parts of the body are always working.
   - ☐ **c.** the blood has more oxygen at night than it does during the day.

2. It is probably true that
   - ☐ **a.** the tongue is the most important organ in the digestive system.
   - ☐ **b.** for an organ system to work well, each organ must do its job.
   - ☐ **c.** scientists now know exactly how the human body works.

3. From the article, you can conclude that
   - ☐ **a.** every cell in the body needs every other cell.
   - ☐ **b.** most people lack the digestive liquids that break down food.
   - ☐ **c.** if one organ does not work, other organs may not be able to survive.

4. If a certain area of a person's body stopped getting blood,
   - ☐ **a.** the tissues in the area would survive on stored oxygen for two or three weeks.
   - ☐ **b.** that person might have a heart attack.
   - ☐ **c.** the cells, tissues, and organs within that area would die.

5. From the article, you can conclude that a part of the body that is made up of one type of tissue
   - ☐ **a.** is an organ.
   - ☐ **b.** is not an organ.
   - ☐ **c.** has at least three kinds of cells.

C. Reading Strategies

1. Recognizing Words in Context

Find the word *grouped* in the article. One definition below is closest to the meaning of that word. One definition has the opposite or nearly the opposite meaning. The remaining definition has a meaning that has nothing to do with the other two words. Label the definitions **C** for *closest,* **O** for *opposite* or *nearly opposite,* and **U** for *unrelated.*

_____ **a.** separated

_____ **b.** moved

_____ **c.** brought together

2. Distinguishing Fact from Opinion

Two of the statements below present *facts,* which can be proved. The other statement is an *opinion,* which expresses someone's thoughts or beliefs. Label the statements **F** for *fact* and **O** for *opinion.*

_____ **a.** The human body cannot survive without its vital organs.

_____ **b.** More people should become scientists to study the human body.

_____ **c.** The digestive system is an organ system because it contains many organs that work together.

3. Making Correct Inferences

Two of the statements below are correct *inferences,* or reasonable guesses, that are based on information in the article. The other statement is an incorrect inference. Label the statements **C** for *correct* inference and **I** for *incorrect* inference.

_____ **a.** There are billions of cells in the human body.

_____ **b.** We could survive without lungs.

_____ **c.** The heart is one of the most important organs in the body.

4. Understanding Main Ideas

One of the statements below expresses the main idea of the article. Another statement is too general, or too broad. The other explains only part of the article; it is too narrow. Label the statements **M** for *main idea,* **B** for *too broad,* and **N** for *too narrow.*

_____ **a.** The human body is filled with amazing organs and organ systems.

_____ **b.** Cells, tissues, and organs work in our bodies to keep us alive and healthy.

_____ **c.** Undigested food moves from the small intestine into the large intestine.

5. Responding to the Article

Complete the following sentence in your own words:

What interested me most in "The Organs of the Body" was

_____

_____

D. Expanding Vocabulary

Content-Area Words

Complete each analogy with a word from the box. Write in the missing word.

| cells | tissues | oxygen | carbon dioxide | intestine |

1. heart : blood :: _____ : food

2. carbon dioxide : breathing out :: _____ : breathing in

3. elephants : big :: _____ : tiny

4. bunches : grapes :: _____ : cells

5. oxygen : inhale :: _____ : exhale

Academic English

In the article "The Organs of the Body," you learned that *distributes* means "divides (something) among people or things." *Distributes* can also mean "spreads or scatters," as in the following sentence.

A gardener distributes vegetable seeds throughout the garden.

Complete the sentence below.

1. One sneeze *distributes* thousands of germs around _____

Now use the word *distributes* in a sentence of your own.

2. _____

_____

You also learned that *transforms* means "changes the way something looks, behaves, or is built." *Transforms* can be used to describe the way the body changes food into energy. *Transforms* can also be used to describe the way other things change, as in the following sentence.

A cocoon transforms a caterpillar into a butterfly.

Complete the sentence below.

3. Cold weather *transforms* the surface of the lake into _____

Now use the word *transforms* in two sentences of your own.

4. _____

5. _____

 Share your new sentences with a partner.

Before You Read

 Think about what you know. Read the title and the first line of the article on the opposite page. Can you think of a physical problem that has made life harder for you—or for someone you know—than it is for other people?

Vocabulary

The content-area and academic English words below appear in "Technology: Overcoming Handicaps." Read the definitions and the example sentences.

Content-Area Words

impairment (im pār′mənt) a problem, sometimes caused by injury, that makes it difficult or impossible to do something without help
Example: Because of a hearing *impairment,* she cannot hear the telephone ring.

devices (di vīs′əz) inventions or machines made for specific reasons
Example: Smoke detectors are *devices* that warn us that fire may be nearby.

waves (wāvz) vibrations that move through the air without being seen
Example: Our voices cause sound *waves* to move through the air.

signals (sig′nəlz) information sent in a way that does not rely on the voice
Example: A remote-control tool sends *signals* to a television set.

keyboard (kē′bôrd′) an arrangement of buttons, called keys, that are used for typing
Example: Even young children can often use a computer *keyboard* to type their names.

Academic English

technology (tek nol′ə jē) scientific knowledge or inventions that make processes simpler
Example: New *technology* has resulted in cameras that are smaller and easier to use than they were before.

display (dis plā′) to show information in a way that people can see easily
Example: Artists want to *display* their paintings in museums where many people will see them.

Rate each vocabulary word according to the following scale. Write a number next to each content-area and academic English word.

4   I have never seen the word before.

3   I have seen the word but do not know what it means.

2   I know what the word means when I read it.

1   I use the word myself in speaking or writing.

 Now skim the article and look for other words that are new to you. Write each new word and its definition in the Personal Dictionary.

While You Read

 Think about why you read. Do you know anyone with a visual or hearing impairment? As you read, look for sentences that tell about machines that people with impairments use every day.

Technology: Overcoming Handicaps

1 When a person cannot hear very well or is deaf, we say that he or she has a hearing **impairment.** New **technology,** or inventions, can help people with hearing problems. Technology uses science to make **devices** that do useful things.

Many people with hearing problems wear hearing aids. A hearing aid is a small
5 device that gets power from a battery. The hearing aid turns sound **waves** into electrical **signals.** It then sends the signals to speakers that turn the waves into sounds loud enough for a hearing-impaired person to hear. Special **keyboard** devices allow people with hearing impairments to use the telephone. When the telephone rings, these devices **display** the words that the person cannot hear but
10 can read. An answer can then be typed on a keyboard and sent to the caller. When the telephone rings, a light flashes.

Alarms have been invented for people with hearing problems. A fire alarm or an alarm clock makes a light flash when a person is awake and makes a pillow vibrate, or shake, when he or she is asleep. An alarm can also have a loud buzzer.

15 Technology lets people with hearing problems enjoy movies and television at home. With technology called closed captioning, words at the bottom of a screen, or captions, spell out what is being said. This technology allows hearing-impaired people to understand a program or a movie. Captioning shows actors' words on the screen so that someone can read them instead of hearing them.

20 Technology also can help people who are visually impaired—those who are unable to see well or to see at all. We say that someone who cannot see at all is blind. A screen reader helps a blind person use a computer. The screen reader reads the screen and speaks the words in a voice that sounds human. Other computers make the words on the screen larger and easier to read.

25 Braille is language that helps a blind person read and write raised dots with the fingers. The dots stand for letters and words. A Braillewriter is a machine that types in Braille. The user presses buttons that make the dots on special paper. Note takers that talk also use Braille. A person writes by pressing buttons on the keyboard. The note taker reads the words aloud or prints them in Braille.

30 A new technology for visually impaired people uses signs that talk. Small machines that send out signals are placed on streets or in buildings. A person holds a device and points it in a direction to learn about that area. For example, when the device is pointed one way, it might speak the word *restroom*. When pointed in another direction, the device might speak the word *stairs*. San Francisco, in
35 California, is one of the cities that has these signs at work.

LANGUAGE CONNECTION

Speakers change sound waves into sounds that you can understand. Music you hear from the radio comes out of speakers. What other things have speakers?

CONTENT CONNECTION

Captions come to television sets as signals. A decoder, a device inside the set, turns the signals into captions. How might closed-captioning technology also help people who are *not* hearing impaired?

After You Read

A. Organizing Ideas

How does technology help people with impairments? Complete the chart below. In the left column, write the name of a device that helps people. In the right column, write a sentence about how that device helps a person. Some blocks have been done for you.

System or Device	How It Helps People
closed captioning	
	has speakers that turn sound waves into sounds a hearing-impaired person can hear
keyboard for the telephone	
	make lights flash and cause beds and pillows to vibrate or buzz very loudly so that a person notices fire alarms or alarm clocks
screen reader	
	lets a blind person read and write by feeling or making groups of raised dots that stand for letters and words

What did you learn about the technology that helps people with impairments after completing this chart? Write two or more sentences about one or two of the devices listed on your chart. Did this chart make the information easy to understand? Explain your answer.

_____

_____

_____

_____

B. Comprehension Skills

 Think about how to find answers. Look back at different parts of the text. What facts help you figure out how to complete the sentences?

Mark box **a, b,** or **c** with an **X** before the choice that best completes each sentence.

Recalling Facts

1. A hearing aid
   - ☐ **a.** changes sound waves into electrical signals.
   - ☐ **b.** gives a person perfect hearing.
   - ☐ **c.** is used only by older people.

2. A person with a hearing impairment can be warned about a fire by
   - ☐ **a.** the sound of fire engines.
   - ☐ **b.** the sound of a smoke detector.
   - ☐ **c.** a flashing light.

3. Braille
   - ☐ **a.** can make the words on a computer screen larger.
   - ☐ **b.** uses raised dots that can be read with the fingers.
   - ☐ **c.** is a kind of hearing aid.

4. Talking note takers
   - ☐ **a.** can read words aloud or print them in Braille.
   - ☐ **b.** are used by the hearing impaired.
   - ☐ **c.** are used on telephones.

5. Signs that talk
   - ☐ **a.** are special fire alarms.
   - ☐ **b.** send out signals that are picked up by a handheld device.
   - ☐ **c.** allow a person who is blind to use a computer.

Understanding Ideas

1. From the article, you can conclude that
   - ☐ **a.** technology has helped more people with hearing impairments than those with visual impairments.
   - ☐ **b.** technology can help only a few people who have hearing problems.
   - ☐ **c.** many devices make life easier for people with hearing or vision problems.

2. In the future, it is most likely that
   - ☐ **a.** all computers will print in Braille.
   - ☐ **b.** computers will have more features for people with disabilities.
   - ☐ **c.** people with impairments will not need guide dogs for help anymore.

3. A person who is hearing impaired will probably get the most help from
   - ☐ **a.** a device that allows him or her to talk on the phone.
   - ☐ **b.** a hearing aid.
   - ☐ **c.** talking signs.

4. A blind person who wants to walk around safely in a city would be helped most by
   - ☐ **a.** talking signs.
   - ☐ **b.** a screen reader.
   - ☐ **c.** a hearing aid.

5. The only one of the following things that does not use technology is
   - ☐ **a.** a flashing fire alarm.
   - ☐ **b.** a talking watch.
   - ☐ **c.** sign language.

C. Reading Strategies

1. Recognizing Words in Context

Find the word *display* in the article. One definition below is closest to the meaning of that word. One definition has the opposite or nearly the opposite meaning. The remaining definition has a meaning that has nothing to do with the other two words. Label the definitions **C** for *closest*, **O** for *opposite* or *nearly opposite*, and **U** for *unrelated*.

_____ **a.** hide

_____ **b.** switch

_____ **c.** show

2. Distinguishing Fact from Opinion

Two of the statements below present *facts*, which can be proved. The other statement is an *opinion*, which expresses someone's thoughts or beliefs. Label the statements **F** for *fact* and **O** for *opinion*.

_____ **a.** Closed captioning is the most important kind of technology for someone with a hearing impairment.

_____ **b.** Hearing aids can help people who have hearing problems to hear sounds.

_____ **c.** Blind people use their fingers to read Braille.

3. Making Correct Inferences

Two of the statements below are correct *inferences*, or reasonable guesses, that are based on information in the article. The other statement is an incorrect inference. Label the statements **C** for *correct* inference and **I** for *incorrect inference*.

_____ **a.** Braille would be useful to deaf people.

_____ **b.** Technology helps keep people with hearing and vision impairments safe.

_____ **c.** Technology can help a blind person find his or her way around a city.

4. Understanding Main Ideas

One of the statements below expresses the main idea of the article. Another statement is too general, or too broad. The other explains only part of the article; it is too narrow. Label the statements **M** for *main idea*, **B** for *too broad*, and **N** for *too narrow*.

_____ **a.** Technology has helped people build many devices that help those with physical impairments to communicate and to stay safe.

_____ **b.** Talking note takers can read words aloud or print them in Braille.

_____ **c.** Devices help blind and deaf people in many ways.

5. Responding to the Article

Complete the following sentence in your own words:

Before reading "Technology: Overcoming Handicaps," I already knew

_____

_____

D. Expanding Vocabulary

Content-Area Words

Complete each sentence with a word from the box. Write the missing word on the line.

| devices | waves | signals | impairment | keyboard |

1. Hearing-impaired people can use a _____ device for the telephone.

2. Technology may help a person who has a physical _____.

3. Sounds travel through the air in invisible _____.

4. Vibrating alarm clocks and fire alarms are _____ that can wake a hearing-impaired person from sleep.

5. A hearing aid changes electrical _____ into sounds a person can hear.

Academic English

In the article "Technology: Overcoming Handicaps," you learned that *technology* means "scientific knowledge or inventions that make processes simpler." *Technology* can apply to aids for people who have hearing or visual impairments. *Technology* can also apply to other inventions or systems, as in the following sentence.

Cell-phone technology helps people talk to each other outside their homes.

Complete the sentence below.

1. I use computer *technology* to help me _____

Now use the word *technology* in a sentence of your own.

2. _____

You also learned that *display* means "to show information in a way that people can see easily." *Display* can also be a noun meaning "something that people can see clearly," as in the following sentence.

There is a new display of modern art at the museum.

Complete the sentence below.

3. A *display* of cakes for sale can be found at a_____

Now use the word *display* in two sentences of your own.

4. _____

5. _____

 Share your new sentences with a partner.

Before You Read

Tip! **Think about what you know.** Read the first and last sentences of the article on the opposite page. What do you think the article might be about?

Vocabulary

The content-area and academic English words below appear in "Vitamins and Minerals: Diet Basics." Read the definitions and the example sentences.

Content-Area Words

antioxidants (an'tē äk'sə dənts) substances that work against the harm that oxygen can do to the body

> *Example:* The *antioxidants* found in strawberries protect our bodies from dangerous substances.

compounds (kom'poundz') mixtures or combinations of two or more ingredients

> *Example:* The scientist mixed chemicals to form *compounds.*

vessels (ves'əlz) tubes, such as veins, that carry blood or other body fluids

> *Example:* The doctor fixed her torn *vessels* so blood could flow through her arm again.

infections (in fek'shənz) illnesses or problems that result when harmful living things, such as germs, enter the body

> *Example:* When we wash our hands, we remove harmful germs that may cause *infections.*

osteoporosis (os'tē ō pə rō'səs) a disease that causes weak bones

> *Example:* I eat foods that contain calcium to avoid bone diseases like *osteoporosis.*

Academic English

function (fungk'shən) to work properly

> *Example:* The car cannot *function* without gasoline and oil.

adequate (ad'ə kwət) enough to meet a specific need or goal

> *Example:* On summer mornings, a sweater is *adequate* to keep a person warm.

Complete the sentences below that contain the content-area and academic English words above. Use the spaces provided. The first one has been done for you.

1. *Antioxidants* help our bodies by preventing <u>oxygen from harming us</u>_____.
2. When a television set *functions*, it _____.
3. Chemical *compounds* are mixtures of _____.
4. Our food was *adequate* for our camping trip because _____.
5. Germs can cause *infections* when they _____.
6. Blood *vessels* work by carrying _____.
7. *Osteoporosis* affects our bones by _____.

Dictionary Now skim the article and look for other words that are new to you. Write each new word and its definition in the Personal Dictionary.

While You Read

 Think about why you read. Everyone should eat foods that are full of vitamins and minerals. As you read, look for the names of foods that contain important vitamins and minerals.

Vitamins and Minerals: Diet Basics

1 Vitamins and minerals are important parts of the human diet, or the foods we eat. The body needs vitamins and minerals to grow and work well. Vitamins help control the chemicals that make energy and living groups of cells, known as tissues. Minerals help parts of the body grow and **function** properly. They also
5 help make some important liquids, such as digestive juices, which help the body break down food. Many vitamins and minerals cannot be made by the body. So humans must get them from the food they eat.

Some foods give us more vitamins and minerals than others do. Fruits and vegetables, for example, are full of vitamins. People who think they are not
10 getting enough vitamins may take vitamin pills. Taking vitamin pills is usually not dangerous, but the best way to get vitamins into your body is by eating a diet that includes many different healthful foods.

Two of the best vitamins are vitamins C and E. These two vitamins are sometimes called **antioxidants** because they protect our tissues from harm that
15 can be caused by some oxygen **compounds.** Vitamin C also helps build strong bones and healthy blood **vessels.** Foods that are good sources of vitamin C include citrus fruits like oranges and grapefruit, strawberries, and tomatoes. Foods made with whole grains such as wheat and oats have a great deal of vitamin E and several of the B vitamins.

20 Another important vitamin is vitamin A. This vitamin keeps skin healthy, helps bones grow, and works to fight **infections.** Eggs and milk have a lot of vitamin A. Orange and dark green vegetables provide beta carotene, which the body can change into vitamin A. You should not eat really big amounts of vitamins A and E.

One of the most important minerals is calcium. Calcium is a mineral that people
25 need for strong bones. If the body does not get **adequate** calcium, it might get a bone disease called **osteoporosis.** Milk and other dairy products have a lot of calcium.

Other important minerals include magnesium, phosphorus, and potassium. Like calcium, magnesium and phosphorus help build strong bones. Whole-grain cereals have a lot of both magnesium and phosphorus. Potassium helps the body hold the
30 right amount of water, and it helps muscles work well. Bananas and oranges are rich in potassium.

There are many other vitamins and minerals that are important for good health. Eating fresh foods rather than foods that are made ahead of time is the best way to get the vitamins and minerals your body needs. Eating unhealthful foods can
35 cause you to become very sick and unhealthy.

CONTENT CONNECTION

Too much of some vitamins and minerals can damage the body. Too much vitamin A can weaken bones. Too much iron can cause liver problems. Most people get enough vitamin A and iron from the foods they eat. What vitamins and minerals do you think you get enough of? Which do you need more of?

LANGUAGE CONNECTION

What may it mean to say that a certain food is *rich in* vitamins or minerals?

After You Read

A. Organizing Ideas

What have you learned about vitamins and minerals? Complete the chart below. In the *What?* column, write the name of an important vitamin or mineral. In the *How?* column, write one or two sentences about how the vitamin or mineral helps our bodies. In the *Where?* column, write where we can find these vitamins or minerals. Use the article to help you. Some boxes have been done for you.

What?	How?	Where?
vitamin C	It works as an antioxidant to protect our bodies from oxygen compounds. It helps build healthy blood vessels and strong bones.	oranges grapefruit strawberries tomatoes
	It works as an antioxidant to protect our bodies from oxygen compounds.	
vitamin A		
		milk dairy products
magnesium		
	It helps build strong bones.	
		oranges bananas

Did completing this chart help you understand the information? Write one or more sentences to explain how the chart helped you. Besides this chart, what other means could you use to organize this information?

_____

_____

_____

B. Comprehension Skills

 Think about how to find answers. Look back at what you read. The information is in the text, but you may have to look in several sentences to find it.

Mark box **a, b,** or **c** with an **X** before the choice that best competes each sentence.

Recalling Facts

1. The best way to get enough vitamins and minerals is to
   - ☐ **a.** take vitamin pills.
   - ☐ **b.** eat a balanced diet.
   - ☐ **c.** eat plenty of meat.

2. Some of the most important vitamins are
   - ☐ **a.** A, C, and E.
   - ☐ **b.** C, K, and M.
   - ☐ **c.** A, E, and G.

3. One mineral that the body uses is
   - ☐ **a.** vitamin C.
   - ☐ **b.** potassium.
   - ☐ **c.** gold.

4. A food that contains a lot of vitamin C is
   - ☐ **a.** chicken.
   - ☐ **b.** carrots.
   - ☐ **c.** strawberries.

5. A food that contains a lot of calcium is
   - ☐ **a.** potatoes.
   - ☐ **b.** pork.
   - ☐ **c.** milk.

Understanding Ideas

1. From the article, you can conclude that vitamins and minerals are needed
   - ☐ **a.** mainly for strong bones.
   - ☐ **b.** for all parts of the body.
   - ☐ **c.** for skin and bones.

2. You can also conclude that some of the most nutritious foods are
   - ☐ **a.** dark green vegetables.
   - ☐ **b.** white breads and rolls.
   - ☐ **c.** french fries and soft drinks.

3. A person who does not like to go to the dentist should have lots of
   - ☐ **a.** milk.
   - ☐ **b.** meat.
   - ☐ **c.** potatoes.

4. From the article, you can conclude that strong and healthy bodies need
   - ☐ **a.** vitamins only.
   - ☐ **b.** minerals only.
   - ☐ **c.** both vitamins and minerals.

5. You can also conclude that, to stay healthy, people should eat
   - ☐ **a.** more vegetables than fruits.
   - ☐ **b.** both fruits and vegetables.
   - ☐ **c.** more fruits than vegetables.

C. Reading Strategies

1. Recognizing Words in Context

Find the word *healthful* in the article. One definition below is closest to the meaning of that word. One definition has the opposite or nearly the opposite meaning. The remaining definition has a meaning that has nothing to do with the other two words. Label the definitions **C** for *closest*, **O** for *opposite* or *nearly opposite*, and **U** for *unrelated*.

_____ **a.** colorful

_____ **b.** bad for the body

_____ **c.** good for the body

2. Distinguishing Fact from Opinion

Two of the statements below present *facts*, which can be proved. The other statement is an *opinion*, which expresses someone's thoughts or beliefs. Label the statements **F** for *fact* and **O** for *opinion*.

_____ **a.** Vitamin C is found in some of the most delicious foods.

_____ **b.** Eating healthful food is the best way to get vitamins and minerals.

_____ **c.** Without enough calcium, bones can develop osteoporosis.

3. Making Correct Inferences

Two of the statements below are correct *inferences*, or reasonable guesses, that are based on information in the article. The other statement is an incorrect, or faulty, inference. Label the statements **C** for *correct* inference and **I** for *incorrect* inference.

_____ **a.** Many vitamins protect the body and help it heal itself.

_____ **b.** Taking a vitamin pill is easier than eating a balanced diet and is just as healthful.

_____ **c.** Too much vitamin A is not healthful.

4. Understanding Main Ideas

One of the statements below expresses the main idea of the article. Another statement is too general, or too broad. The other explains only part of the article; it is too narrow. Label the statements **M** for *main idea*, **B** for *too broad*, and **N** for *too narrow*.

_____ **a.** Potassium helps muscles work well.

_____ **b.** The body needs vitamins and minerals.

_____ **c.** Vitamins and minerals, found in many healthful foods, are necessary to keep the body working well.

5. Responding to the Article

Complete the following sentences in your own words:

One thing I did best while reading "Vitamins and Minerals: Diet Basics" was

_____

I think that I did this well because _____

D. Expanding Vocabulary

Content-Area Words

Read each item carefully. Write on the line the word or phrase that best completes
each sentence.

1. Antioxidants help protect our tissues from damage caused by too much _____ .

    carbon   oxygen   hydrogen

2. _____ moves through your body in vessels such as veins and arteries.

    Water   Juice   Blood

3. The vitamin _____ in eggs and milk helps your body fight infections.

    C   M   A

4. To prevent osteoporosis, eat foods high in calcium, such as _____ .

    milk and cheese   chocolate and nuts   oranges and lemons

5. Vitamins C and E protect us from _____ compounds that contain too
much oxygen.

    harmful   easy   beautiful

Academic English

In the article "Vitamins and Minerals: Diet Basics," you learned that *function* is a
verb that means "to work properly." *Function* can also be a noun that means "purpose
or reason that a job is done," as in the following sentence.

    The function of a fan is to move air and keep people cool.

Complete the sentence below.

1. The *function* of a chair is to provide a place to _____

Now use the word *function* in a sentence of your own.

2. _____

You also learned that *adequate* means "enough to meet a specific need or goal."
Adequate can also mean "barely enough," as in the following sentence.

    His grades were adequate, but they were not what he had hoped for.

Complete the sentence below.

3. The money they had was *adequate* to live on, but it was not enough to pay for _____

Now use the word *adequate* in two sentences of your own.

4. _____

5. _____

 Share your new sentences with a partner.

Gymnastics: A Sport of Balance

Before You Read

Tip! **Think about what you know.** Read the title and the first two sentences of the article on the opposite page. Have you ever seen the sport of gymnastics at school or on television? What impressed you most about the sport?

Vocabulary

The content-area and academic English words below appear in "Gymnastics: A Sport of Balance." Read the definitions and the example sentences.

Content-Area Words

gymnastics (jim nas'tiks) physical exercises that help someone develop strength and balance
  Example: Sam did *gymnastics* every day, and his body became very strong.

flexible (flek'sə bəl) able to bend and twist easily
  Example: I am *flexible* enough to touch my toes without bending my knees.

apparatus (ap'ə rat'əs) a set of equipment used for something specific
  Example: Weights are my favorite *apparatus* at the gym.

nerves (nurvz) tiny, ropelike bands of tissue that carry electrical impulses between the brain and the spinal cord and to other parts of the body
  Example: *Nerves* in my hand tell me that the stove is hot.

springboard (spring'bôrd') a flexible board, usually fastened to something solid at one end, that is used for jumping high in gymnastics or diving
  Example: He jumped on the *springboard,* flew high in the air, and dove into the swimming pool.

Academic English

contract (kən trakt') to tighten or draw together
  Example: She felt her arm muscles *contract* when she lifted the heavy bag.

adjustment (ə just'mənt) a change made in order to fix a problem
  Example: The mechanic made an *adjustment* to the engine, and now the car runs well.

Read again the example sentences that follow the content-area and academic English word definitions. With a partner, discuss the meanings of the words and sentences. Then make up a sentence of your own for each word.

 Now skim the article and look for other words that are new to you. Write each new word and its definition in the Personal Dictionary.

While You Read

 Think about why you read. Have you ever balanced yourself on a balance beam? As you read, think about why balancing is important for people who do gymnastics.

Gymnastics
A Sport of Balance

1 To be good at the sport of **gymnastics,** you must be able to control the shape, motion, and position of your body. Gymnasts, or people who do gymnastics, work very hard to get stronger and more **flexible.** Their strength and flexibility allow them to pose, or keep their bodies very still, in a certain way. Strength and
5 flexibility also allow them to change their positions on the floor as well as on **apparatus** like bars, beams, and rings.

Even someone who works very hard at gymnastics will not do well without balance. It is a very important part of this sport. Balance is a natural skill of the body that is controlled by the brain. The brain gets information from **nerves**
10 throughout the body. It uses this information to help the body move so as to stay balanced. Joints, such as shoulders, knees, and elbows, also help with balance. So do muscles, the skin, the eyes, and—especially—the inner part of the ear.

As a gymnast performs, or does gymnastics, the brain has to tell the rest of the body very quickly what changes in movement to make to stay balanced. It sends
15 electric messages called signals through the nerves to certain muscles. The signals cause muscles to **contract,** or tighten. As a muscle contracts, it pulls on a bone. This action causes a part of the body, such as an arm or a leg, to move. The brain determines which bones move and how much they should move.

Vaulting is one type of gymnastics that shows how nerves and the brain work
20 together to control balance. When a gymnast vaults, he or she first runs toward a **springboard** and jumps onto it. The springboard then pushes the gymnast toward a wide, padded horizontal beam called a horse. The horse is about 1.2 meters (47.2 inches) or 1.35 meters (53.1 inches) high. As the gymnast comes off the springboard, the brain tells the arms and legs where to go to stay balanced. Nerves
25 along the joints and muscles send information to the brain about the body's location in the air. The brain then sends signals out if an **adjustment** needs to be made. The brain uses information from the eyes to control exactly where the gymnast's hands should go on the horse. As the hands touch the horse, nerves in the skin give the brain more information about the body's position. This
30 information may tell whether the body is leaning to the left or the right. The brain directs the hands to push off the horse and into the air, where the gymnast does twists or other movements.

The gymnast must end up standing on a mat. Landing well requires special balance. The movement of the liquid found inside the inner ear sends nerve
35 signals that help the brain rebalance the body into a standing position.

LANGUAGE CONNECTION

A pronoun takes the place of a noun in a sentence to avoid repeating the noun. A pronoun must agree with its antecedent, or the word that the pronoun is to replace, in number and gender. The singular neuter pronoun *it* appears twice in the second paragraph. To what word does *it* refer in each case?

CONTENT CONNECTION

Nerves keep our bodies safe. If you touch a hot pan or a sharp knife, nerves send signals to your brain. Your brain sends signals back to your muscles. You then move your hand away from the pan or knife. How have your nerves helped keep you safe today?

After You Read

A. Organizing Ideas

What happens in your body to help you keep your balance? Think about what your body does to stay balanced. List these steps in order in the chart below. Inside each box, write one or two sentences about the step. Refer to the article for help. The first box has been done for you.

The Steps for Staying Balanced

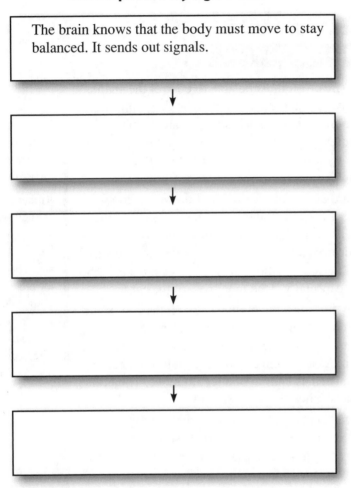

The brain knows that the body must move to stay balanced. It sends out signals.

How did this chart help you understand the work your body does to stay balanced? Write two or more sentences about how this chart helped you organize the body's work into steps. Would you use this type of chart again? Explain your answer.

_____

_____

_____

_____

B. Comprehension Skills

 Think about how to find answers. Think about what each sentence means. Try to say it to yourself in your own words before you complete it.

Mark box **a, b,** or **c** with an **X** before the choice that best completes each sentence.

Recalling Facts

1. Gymnasts practice a lot to increase their
   - ☐ **a.** height and muscle tone.
   - ☐ **b.** nerve sensitivity and brain chemistry.
   - ☐ **c.** strength and flexibility.

2. The part of the body that controls balance is
   - ☐ **a.** the spine.
   - ☐ **b.** the brain.
   - ☐ **c.** the eye.

3. Information about the body's location is sent to the brain from
   - ☐ **a.** the heart.
   - ☐ **b.** the ground.
   - ☐ **c.** nerves throughout the body.

4. Equipment used in gymnastics includes
   - ☐ **a.** beams, bars, and rings.
   - ☐ **b.** ropes, hoops, and poles.
   - ☐ **c.** trapezes, tightropes, and nets.

5. The brain receives information from nerves in the inner ear according to the movement of
   - ☐ **a.** wax in the ear canal.
   - ☐ **b.** cells in the eardrum.
   - ☐ **c.** liquid in ear passageways.

Understanding Ideas

1. Gymnasts work hard to develop muscles
   - ☐ **a.** in all parts of the body.
   - ☐ **b.** mainly in the arms.
   - ☐ **c.** mainly in the legs.

2. From the article, you can conclude that, over time, a gymnast's sense of balance
   - ☐ **a.** stays about the same.
   - ☐ **b.** gets a little bit worse.
   - ☐ **c.** gets better.

3. It is likely that the most dangerous part of a vault is when the gymnast
   - ☐ **a.** is running up to the springboard.
   - ☐ **b.** is pushing off the horse.
   - ☐ **c.** has landed on the mat.

4. From the article, you can conclude that the whole process of performing a vault takes
   - ☐ **a.** less than one second.
   - ☐ **b.** several seconds.
   - ☐ **c.** about a minute.

5. To keep the body's balance during vaulting, the brain uses information from
   - ☐ **a.** only the inner ear.
   - ☐ **b.** only the arms and legs.
   - ☐ **c.** several parts of the body.

C. Reading Strategies

1. Recognizing Words in Context

Find the word *determines* in the article. One definition below is closest to the meaning of that word. One definition has the opposite or nearly the opposite meaning. The remaining definition has a meaning that has nothing to do with the other two words. Label the definitions **C** for *closest,* **O** for *opposite* or *nearly opposite,* and **U** for *unrelated.*

_____ **a.** chooses or picks

_____ **b.** yells or screams

_____ **c.** wonders what to do

2. Distinguishing Fact from Opinion

Two of the statements below present *facts,* which can be proved. The other statement is an *opinion,* which expresses someone's thoughts or beliefs. Label the statements **F** for *fact* and **O** for *opinion.*

_____ **a.** Nerves send information to the brain to help the body move and stay balanced.

_____ **b.** Gymnasts are graceful and entertaining to watch.

_____ **c.** Joints, muscles, skin, eyes, and the inner ear help the body stay balanced.

3. Making Correct Inferences

Two of the statements below are correct *inferences,* or reasonable guesses, that are based on information in the article. The other statement is an incorrect, or faulty, inference. Label the statements **C** for *correct* inference and **I** for *incorrect* inference.

_____ **a.** The brain controls a gymnast's movements and balance.

_____ **b.** A nerve or brain injury would make it difficult to do gymnastics.

_____ **c.** Liquid in the inner ear makes it difficult for a gymnast to hear.

4. Understanding Main Ideas

One of the statements below expresses the main idea of the article. Another statement is too general, or too broad. The other explains only part of the article; it is too narrow. Label the statements **M** for *main idea,* **B** for *too broad,* and **N** for *too narrow.*

_____ **a.** The brain and nerves help control one of the most important parts of doing gymnastics: keeping the body balanced.

_____ **b.** The brain is used in many ways when we exercise.

_____ **c.** Gymnasts use a springboard to do vaulting.

5. Responding to the Article

Complete the following sentences in your own words:

Before I read "Gymnastics: A Sport of Balance," I thought

_____

But now, I know_____

_____

D. Expanding Vocabulary

Content-Area Words

Cross out one word or phrase in each row that is not related to the word in dark type.

1. **gymnastics**	balance	sport	goalpost	flexibility
2. **flexible**	bend	positions	stretch	rest
3. **apparatus**	mat	beam	twist	bars
4. **nerves**	information	signals	direction	brain
5. **springboard**	skate	vault	jump	bounce

Academic English

In the article "Gymnastics: A Sport of Balance," you learned that *contract* means "to tighten or draw together." *Contract* can also mean "to become infected with a disease," as in the following sentence.

> *You may miss a day of school if you contract a cold.*

Complete the sentence below.

1. If you *contract* the flu, you may need to take some _____

Now use the word *contract* in a sentence of your own.

2. _____

_____

You also learned that *adjustment* means "a change made in order to fix a problem." *Adjustment* can also mean "a change made to make something fit," as in the following sentence.

> *The skirt may need an adjustment if it is too loose.*

Complete the sentence below.

3. The carpet did not fit exactly, so an *adjustment* _____

Now use the word *adjustment* in two sentences of your own.

4. _____

5. _____

 Share your new sentences with a partner.

Reading a Brochure

Read the brochure on the benefits of not smoking. Circle the word that completes each sentence.

The Dangers of Smoking

Smoking hurts. Thousands of people die every day from health problems caused by smoking. Consider these common questions about what smoking does.

Q: How do cigarettes affect my lungs?

A: Cigarettes decrease lung (**function, adjustment**) and increase mucus in the lungs. Both of these effects cause smokers to cough and increase their chances to (**contract, establish**) serious infections.

Q: Does smoking affect other parts of my body?

A: Yes. The blood vessels carry oxygen to the cells and (**carbon dioxide, antioxidants**) away from

them. Smoking causes blood vessels to become narrow. Then oxygen cannot reach the billions of cells in your body. Without (**adequate, tissues**) oxygen, some cells die.

Q: How can someone stop smoking?

A: A family doctor can direct smokers to information about breaking the smoking habit. The library (**establish, distributes**) books and pamphlets on the subject too.

Reading an Award Certificate

Read the award certificate. Then complete the sentences. Use words from the Word Bank.

Word Bank

display	author
transforms	honors
document	

Award to the Best _____ of a science book
presented to Fernando Diaz, Ph.D., for his book titled
The World of Butterflies
on this fifteenth day of February, in the year two thousand and seven

This award is one of the greatest _____ for authors of science books.

The book shows how nature _____ a caterpillar into a beautiful butterfly.

This award recognizes the research and creativity of Professor Diaz.

A copy of this _____ will be sent to your university.

It is for you to _____ for all to see. Congratulations!

Making Connections

Work with a partner. Talk about what the words mean. Write down words that go together in one of the columns below. Then write a name for each group of words.

compounds	signals	keyboard	technology	devices
osteoporosis	impairment	intestine	apparatus	tissues

Group 1	Group 2	Group 3
_____	_____	_____
_____	_____	_____
_____	_____	_____
_____	_____	_____

Use all of the words above in complete sentences of your own. Each sentence may include one or more of the words. To help you start writing, think about the groups of words you created. After you write your sentences, read them over. If you find a mistake, correct it.

_____

_____

_____

_____

_____

_____

_____

_____

_____

_____

_____

You *Can* Grow Plants from Seeds

Before You Read

Tip! **Think about what you know.** Read the lesson title above. What do you predict the article will be about? What do you know about growing plants?

Vocabulary

The content-area and academic English words below appear in "You *Can* Grow Plants from Seeds." Read the definitions and the example sentences.

Content-Area Words

conditions (kən dish′ənz) things necessary for the appearance or happening of something
   Example: The rich, moist soil provided the perfect *conditions* for the plants to grow in.

clay (klā) a sticky material found in the earth that can be shaped when it is wet and that gets hard when it is dried or baked
   Example: In my art class, we made flowerpots out of *clay*.

fertilizer (furt′əl ī′zər) nutrients added to the soil to help plants grow
   Example: The farmer spread *fertilizer* onto the field so that the plants would be healthy.

sprout (sprout) to begin to grow
   Example: Many plants *sprout* in the spring.

roots (ro͞ots) the part of a plant that grows downward into the soil and takes in water and food
   Example: The *roots* of large trees go deep into the ground.

Academic English

consult (kən sult′) to seek advice or ideas from someone or something
   Example: You may *consult* a medical book for information about your health.

select (si lekt′) to choose something from a group of choices
   Example: It can be difficult to *select* a meal from a large menu.

Rate each vocabulary word according to the following scale. Write a number next to each content-area and academic English word.

4   I have never seen the word before.

3   I have seen the word but do not know what it means.

2   I know what the word means when I read it.

1   I use the word myself in speaking or writing.

Dictionary Now skim the article and look for other words that are new to you. Write each new word and its definition in the Personal Dictionary.

While You Read

 Think about why you read. Have you ever planted seeds or grown different kinds of plants? As you read, think about what kinds of plants you would grow where you live.

You Can GROW Plants from Seeds

1   Gardening, or growing and caring for plants, can be interesting and fun. Some helpful steps can make it easier to grow seeds in a garden.

Step 1: Find out which plants grow best where you live. For example, some plants that grow well in California cannot grow in Michigan. Ask some good
5   gardeners which plants grow well for them. **Consult** gardening books for ideas. Make a list of interesting plants that grow well in your area. Next to the name of each plant, write down the **conditions** in which it needs to grow.

Step 2: Think about the growing conditions in your garden. Is the dirt (or soil) light and sandy or heavy and full of **clay?** How much sunshine does the garden
10   receive? **Select** plants from the list that need the kind of soil and the amount of sunshine the garden has. For example, impatiens are flowers that grow best in shade, or places that sunlight does not reach. Geraniums are flowers that grow best with sunlight shining on them most of the day.

Step 3: Buy fresh seeds that should be planted this year.

15   *Step 4:* Know the best time of the year to plant. In some southern states, you can plant anytime during the year. In northern states, you should plant in the spring—as soon as it is warm enough and there is little danger of frost. Cold temperatures could cause your plants to freeze. In places where warm, sunny weather does not last very long, plant the seeds indoors in cups of soil. Then place
20   the cups near a sunny window. Vegetables such as tomatoes and peppers, as well as flowers such as zinnias and marigolds, can be grown for a few weeks indoors. They can be transplanted, or moved and put into the ground outdoors, when the weather gets warmer.

Step 5: Prepare the garden for planting by breaking up clumps of dirt. Mix
25   **fertilizer** into the soil. Then rake the ground so that it is smooth.

Step 6: Plant the seeds in rows. Read the directions on the seed packages to find out how deep into the soil and how far apart the seeds should be.

Step 7: Use a small amount of water to keep the soil moist, or slightly wet, until the seeds **sprout.** Then water the plants as often and as much as they need it. For
30   example, zinnias do not need to be watered very often. They need to be watered heavily, however, so that the water can reach down to the deepest **roots.** Other plants, such as begonias, need to be watered lightly every two days. As the plants grow, pull out any nearby weeds, or plants that grow where you do not want them to grow.

Step 8: To help new flowers bloom, cut off the old flowers when they have
35   finished blooming and begin to look faded, or less colorful.

CONTENT CONNECTION

This article tells you in steps how to plant a garden. Steps are instructions that explain what to do in a set order. Where have you seen numbered steps before?

LANGUAGE CONNECTION

The word *transplanted* means "moved from one place to another place." Doctors transplant organs, such as a heart or a kidney, from one person to another. Gardeners transplant plants from pots to the ground outside. Have you heard the word *transplant* before?

After You Read

A. Organizing Ideas

How do you grow your own plants? Complete the web below. In each oval, summarize one of the eight steps for growing plants. Refer to the article to find the steps. The ovals are numbered. The first one has been done for you.

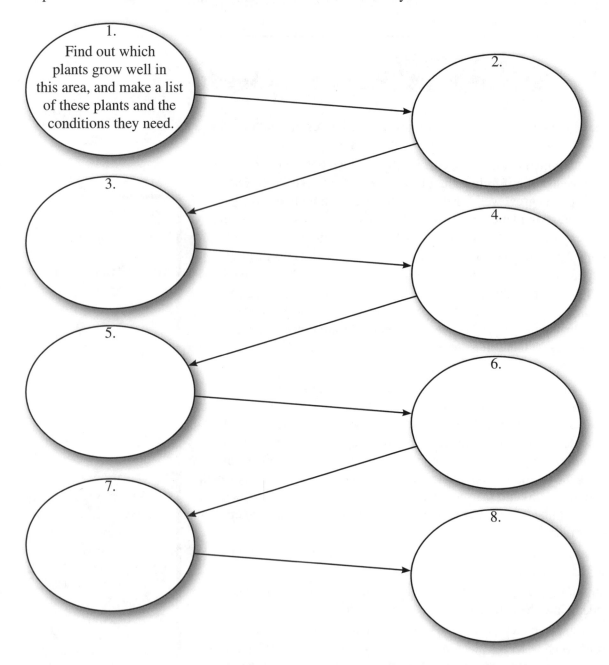

1. Find out which plants grow well in this area, and make a list of these plants and the conditions they need.
2.
3.
4.
5.
6.
7.
8.

What did you learn about the process of growing plants from completing the web? Write two or more sentences about what you learned. Is it easier for you to read directions in text or in a web? Explain your answer.

_____

_____

B. Comprehension Skills

 Think about how to find answers. Think about what each sentence means. Try to say it to yourself in your own words before you complete it.

Mark box **a, b,** or **c** with an **X** before the choice that best completes each sentence.

Recalling Facts

1. A good way to find out which plants will grow best in a garden is to
- ☐ **a.** plant many kinds of seeds and see which ones grow well.
- ☐ **b.** ask gardeners in the neighborhood.
- ☐ **c.** make a list of the plants you like.

2. Important conditions in a garden include everything except
- ☐ **a.** the type of soil.
- ☐ **b.** the age of garden tools.
- ☐ **c.** the amount of sunshine.

3. In the northern states, seeds should be planted
- ☐ **a.** in dry soil.
- ☐ **b.** at many times of the year.
- ☐ **c.** in the spring, as soon as it is warm enough.

4. Before seeds have sprouted, gardeners should
- ☐ **a.** keep the soil moist at all times.
- ☐ **b.** water the soil every two days.
- ☐ **c.** water the soil heavily once a week.

5. When seeds are planted indoors in cups of soil, the cups should be put
- ☐ **a.** on a table in the middle of a room.
- ☐ **b.** in a warm, dark basement.
- ☐ **c.** near a sunny window.

Understanding Ideas

1. To grow plants from seeds, it is most important for a gardener to
- ☐ **a.** plant them in rows.
- ☐ **b.** start growing them in cups.
- ☐ **c.** choose plants that grow well where the gardener lives.

2. In a place that is warm all year, gardeners
- ☐ **a.** can plant seeds outside anytime.
- ☐ **b.** should plant seeds only in the spring.
- ☐ **c.** must plant seeds inside first and then later move the plants outside.

3. From the article, you can conclude that seeds, in order to sprout, must have
- ☐ **a.** expensive fertilizers.
- ☐ **b.** shelter from the wind.
- ☐ **c.** water and warmth.

4. You can also conclude that the word *transplanted,* as it is used in the article, means
- ☐ **a.** "moved a plant from a pot to a garden."
- ☐ **b.** "added pollen to a plant."
- ☐ **c.** "put seeds into a garden."

5. A gardener who plants seeds outdoors in October probably lives in
- ☐ **a.** Michigan.
- ☐ **b.** California.
- ☐ **c.** Alaska.

C. Reading Strategies

1. Recognizing Words in Context

Find the word *clumps* in the article. One definition below is closest to the meaning of that word. One definition has the opposite or nearly the opposite meaning. The remaining definition has a meaning that has nothing to do with the other two words. Label the definitions **C** for *closest,* **O** for *opposite* or *nearly opposite,* and **U** for *unrelated.*

_____ **a.** rows of plants

_____ **b.** lumps of something stuck together

_____ **c.** loose material

2. Distinguishing Fact from Opinion

Two of the statements below present *facts,* which can be proved. The other statement is an *opinion,* which expresses someone's thoughts or beliefs. Label the statements **F** for *fact* and **O** for *opinion.*

_____ **a.** Zinnias are more colorful than marigolds.

_____ **b.** The right time to plant seeds varies throughout the United States.

_____ **c.** Some plants grow best in sunlight, and some grow best in shade.

3. Making Correct Inferences

Two of the statements below are correct *inferences,* or reasonable guesses, that are based on information in the article. The other statement is an incorrect, or faulty, inference. Label the statements **C** for *correct* inference and **I** for *incorrect* inference.

_____ **a.** The roots of a plant grow downward into the soil.

_____ **b.** Weeds that are not pulled may get in the way of other plants.

_____ **c.** It is fine to plant tomatoes anytime, anywhere.

4. Understanding Main Ideas

One of the statements below expresses the main idea of the article. Another statement is too general, or too broad. The other explains only part of the article; it is too narrow. Label the statements **M** for *main idea,* **B** for *too broad,* and **N** for *too narrow.*

_____ **a.** Begonias need to be watered lightly every two days—unlike zinnias, which need to be watered less often.

_____ **b.** A successful garden needs the right seeds and proper conditions in prepared soil.

_____ **c.** Gardening is easy if plants have what they need.

5. Responding to the Article

Complete the following sentences in your own words:

One of the things I did best while reading "You *Can* Grow Plants from Seeds" was

_____

I think that I did this well because _____

_____

D. Expanding Vocabulary

Content-Area Words

Complete each sentence with a word from the box. Write the missing word on the line.

fertilizer	clay	roots	sprout	conditions

1. Before you plant seeds, know what _____ they need in order to grow.

2. If soil has too much _____ in it, plants may not grow well.

3. If growing plants cannot get all the nutrients they need from the soil, they may need _____.

4. It may take only a few days for seeds to _____.

5. If you break the _____ of a plant, it may not be able to take in water.

Academic English

In the article "You *Can* Grow Plants from Seeds," you learned that *consult* means "to seek advice or ideas from someone or something." *Consult* can describe seeking advice from a book. *Consult* can also describe seeking advice or ideas from people or from other places, as in the following sentence.

I could consult my grandfather about life during the 1930s.

Complete the sentence below.

1. If you have questions about your schoolwork, you might *consult* _____

Now use the word *consult* in a sentence of your own.

2. _____

_____

You also learned that *select* is a verb that means "to choose something from a group of choices." *Select* can also be an adjective that means "of special value or excellence," as in the following sentence.

Only a select few were permitted to attend the performance.

Complete the sentence below.

3. The apples sent as a gift were of *select* _____

Now use the word *select* in two sentences of your own.

4. _____

5. _____

 Share your new sentences with a partner.

Before You Read

Tip! **Think about what you know.** Read the title and the first two sentences of the article on the opposite page. What do you already know about the different kinds of precipitation?

_____

Vocabulary

The content-area and academic English words below appear in "Precipitation." Read the definitions and the example sentences.

Content-Area Words

atmosphere (at′məs fēr′) the gases or air that surrounds Earth or any other planet
   Example: Earth's _atmosphere_ contains oxygen that people breathe in.

moisture (mois′chər) water or other liquid in the air
   Example: Rain is _moisture_ that falls from clouds.

crystals (krist′əlz) minerals, with patterns and flat surfaces, that are often clear and transparent
   Example: Snowflakes are _crystals_ of ice that fall from the sky.

humidity (hū mid′ə tē) moisture or dampness of the air that is caused by water vapor
   Example: On very hot days, _humidity_ in the air can make the skin feel sticky.

currents (kur′ənts) directed flows of air, water, or electricity
   Example: A fan blows _currents_ of air into or around a room.

Academic English

attach (ə tach′) to connect or put together
   Example: You can use paper clips to _attach_ several pieces of paper.

potentially (pə ten′shə lē) in a way that seems possible
   Example: Lightning is _potentially_ dangerous.

Complete the sentences below that contain the content-area and academic English words above. Use the spaces provided. The first one has been done for you.

1. Ocean _currents_ flow _in many directions_____.
2. Walking on slippery ice is _potentially_ _____.
3. Too much water in the _atmosphere_ could result in _____.
4. _Crystals_ that have no color are_____.
5. To _attach_ an essay to note cards, you could use_____.
6. Hail and snow are forms of _moisture_ that are_____.
7. Without enough _humidity_, the air will feel_____.

_____

 Now skim the article and look for other words that are new to you. Write each new word and its definition in the Personal Dictionary.

While You Read

Tip! **Think about why you read.** Have you seen all of the different kinds of precipitation? What causes different types of precipitation? As you read, look for the answer.

Precipitation

1   Any water that falls through the **atmosphere** is called precipitation. This water can come down in different ways, such as rain, snow, hail, and sleet.

   We know rain as drops of water that fall from clouds. Warm air picks up tiny drops of **moisture** from Earth's oceans, lakes, rivers, and streams. This moisture
5 is called water vapor. Warm air tends to rise; as it rises, it gets cooler. Since cool air cannot hold as much moisture as warm air can, the water vapor will **attach** to tiny pieces of dirt, dust, or pollen from plants and form small drops, or droplets. These droplets form clouds. As more and more water vapor sticks to the droplets, they become too heavy to float in the air, and they fall as rain.

10   If the temperature is very cold, the water vapor freezes around the bits of dust or pollen and forms **crystals.** As more and more water vapor freezes onto the crystals, they grow into snowflakes. When the snowflakes get heavy enough, they fall to the ground.

   All snow crystals are symmetrical, or have two identical halves. This means
15 that if the crystal were cut in half, each half would be exactly the same. A single snowflake can be made of up to two hundred crystals. Snow crystals have four basic shapes. One looks like a long needle, like one with which you would sew a button on a shirt. This type of crystal forms very high up in the atmosphere, where the air is coldest. The other three shapes are hexagons; that is, they have
20 six sides. One hexagon shape looks like a hollow pole. Another looks flat. The third looks like a star. A crystal gets its shape from the temperature and **humidity** that are part of the air while the crystal forms.

   Hail is balls of ice, called hailstones, that form in layers. Inside storm clouds are wind **currents** that flow upward. These winds carry water droplets up to
25 colder air, where they freeze into tiny pieces of ice. As the pieces of ice begin to fall, the wind currents may push them back up again. Layers of ice are added to these ice pieces until they turn into ice balls. When these balls become too heavy for the winds to lift them, they fall to the ground as hailstones. Most hailstones are smaller than a marble, but some can be much larger.

30   Sleet forms when rain moves through very cold air near the ground and becomes partly frozen. Sleet can cover car windows, telephone wires, and roads. The icy coating formed in this way can make roads **potentially** dangerous.

CONTENT CONNECTION

No two snowflakes are alike. Each is unique, or unlike any other. Have you ever seen a picture of a snowflake that shows its amazing shape?

LANGUAGE CONNECTION

Hexagon comes from the Greek word root *hex*, which means "six." A hexagon has six sides. Can you draw one?

After You Read

A. Organizing Ideas

What are the different forms of precipitation? Complete the chart below. Write a brief definition of each type of precipitation. Then list two important facts about each kind of precipitation. Refer to the article to help you. Some parts have been done for you.

Rain	Snow	Hail	Sleet
			partly frozen moisture that falls from the sky
Fact 1: Rain begins to form when warm air picks up tiny drops of moisture from Earth.	Fact 1:	Fact 1: Hailstones are balls of ice that are formed in layers.	Fact 1:
Fact 2:	Fact 2: All snowflakes are symmetrical.	Fact 2:	Fact 2:

What are the main differences in conditions that cause the types of precipitation? Write two or more sentences about the differences. Did you think the chart helped you to find the differences? In what way?

_____

_____

_____

_____

_____

B. Comprehension Skills

 Think about how to find answers. Look back at what you read. The information is in the text, but you may have to look in several sentences to find it.

Mark box **a, b,** or **c** with an **X** before the choice that best completes each sentence.

Recalling Facts

1. Precipitation is any
   - ☐ **a.** wind that carries water vapor.
   - ☐ **b.** group of clouds high in the atmosphere.
   - ☐ **c.** kind of water that falls through the atmosphere.

2. Rain is made up of
   - ☐ **a.** drops of water that freeze.
   - ☐ **b.** drops of water that melt.
   - ☐ **c.** droplets of water vapor that form a cloud.

3. Three of the types of ice crystals
   - ☐ **a.** are shaped like needles.
   - ☐ **b.** are six-sided and symmetrical.
   - ☐ **c.** have liquid water trapped inside them.

4. Hail is made up of
   - ☐ **a.** balls of ice that are formed in layers.
   - ☐ **b.** clumps of snowflakes.
   - ☐ **c.** fog that freezes.

5. Sleet forms when
   - ☐ **a.** rain hits very cold air near the ground and becomes partly frozen.
   - ☐ **b.** air near the ground can hold no more water vapor.
   - ☐ **c.** snow melts in a cloud.

Understanding Ideas

1. From the article, you can conclude that
   - ☐ **a.** water moves from Earth into the atmosphere and back to the ground again.
   - ☐ **b.** ocean water is beginning to dry up.
   - ☐ **c.** lakes are made of water vapor.

2. You can also conclude that all forms of precipitation do not
   - ☐ **a.** fall from clouds.
   - ☐ **b.** have about the same temperature.
   - ☐ **c.** contain bits of dust and pollen.

3. Very high clouds are likely to be made of
   - ☐ **a.** air and gases.
   - ☐ **b.** ice crystals.
   - ☐ **c.** sleet.

4. If hail the size of golf balls began to fall, you would know that
   - ☐ **a.** the hail formed in clouds with very strong upward wind currents.
   - ☐ **b.** wind pushed hailstones together as they fell from the sky.
   - ☐ **c.** huge hailstones exploded high in the atmosphere.

5. Tree branches are most likely to break when they are covered with a large amount of
   - ☐ **a.** snow.
   - ☐ **b.** rain.
   - ☐ **c.** sleet.

C. Reading Strategies

1. Recognizing Words in Context

Find the word *partly* in the article. One definition below is closest to the meaning of that word. One definition has the opposite or nearly the opposite meaning. The remaining definition has a meaning that has nothing to do with the other two words. Label the definitions **C** for *closest,* **O** for *opposite* or *nearly opposite,* and **U** for *unrelated.*

_____ **a.** completely

_____ **b.** somewhat or sort of

_____ **c.** inclined to be fat

2. Distinguishing Fact from Opinion

Two of the statements below present *facts,* which can be proved. The other statement is an *opinion,* which expresses someone's thoughts or beliefs. Label the statements **F** for *fact* and **O** for *opinion.*

_____ **a.** One snowflake may be made of up to two hundred ice crystals.

_____ **b.** Cool air cannot hold as much moisture or water vapor as warm air can.

_____ **c.** Hail can damage cars more than sleet can.

3. Making Correct Inferences

Two of the statements below are correct *inferences,* or reasonable guesses, that are based on information in the article. The other statement is an incorrect, or faulty, inference. Label the statements **C** for *correct* inference and **I** for *incorrect* inference.

_____ **a.** Large hailstones have many layers of ice on them.

_____ **b** Earth's oceans and lakes supply the water that falls down as rain.

_____ **c.** Sleet is made of melting snow crystals.

4. Understanding Main Ideas

One of the statements below expresses the main idea of the article. Another statement is too general, or too broad. The other explains only part of the article; it is too narrow. Label the statements **M** for *main idea,* **B** for *too broad,* and **N** for *too narrow.*

_____ **a.** The forms of precipitation we call snow, rain, hail, and sleet each form in a different way.

_____ **b.** Wind currents flow upward within storm clouds, and this causes hail to form.

_____ **c.** Water falls through the atmosphere in many forms.

5. Responding to the Article

Complete the following sentence in your own words:
One thing in "Precipitation" that I cannot understand is

_____

_____

D. Expanding Vocabulary

Content-Area Words

Read each item carefully. Write on the line the word or phrase that best completes each sentence.

1. Rain, sleet, snow, and hail that fall through Earth's atmosphere are _____.
   weather   precipitation   storms

2. Warm air that picks up moisture from a lake is called_____.
   water bottle   water cloud   water vapor

3. There are_____ basic types of snow crystals.
   four   three   five

4. _____ and humidity cause the shape of a snow crystal.
   Temperature   Hail   Weight

5. Wind currents flow_____within storm clouds.
   sideways   upward   downward

Academic English

In the article "Precipitation," you learned that *attach* means "to connect or put together." *Attach* can relate to how water vapor connects to tiny items in the air to make rain. *Attach* can also mean "to connect in ties of affection," as in the following sentence.

   A puppy may attach itself to a human being as it would to its mother.

Complete the sentence below.

1. The members of a family *attach* themselves to _____

Now use the word *attach* in a sentence of your own.

2. _____

You also learned that *potentially* means "in a way that seems possible." *Potentially* can relate to possible dangers. *Potentially* can also relate to positive things that are possible, as in the following sentence.

   Eating citrus fruits could potentially protect sailors from scurvy.

Complete the sentence below.

3. Farmers look for clouds in the sky that might *potentially* _____

Now use the word *potentially* in two sentences of your own.

4. _____

5. _____

 Share your new sentences with a partner.

Before You Read

Tip! **Think about what you know.** Skim the article on the opposite page. Can you explain why colors appear the way they do?

Vocabulary

The content-area and academic English words below appear in "Why Is the Ocean Blue?" Read the definitions and the example sentences.

Content-Area Words

reflects (ri flekts′) throws or gives back waves of light, heat, or sound
  Example: A mirror *reflects* your image.

absorbs (ab sôrbz′) takes in and holds or keeps without any reflection
  Example: A towel *absorbs* the water on your skin after you swim.

particles (pär′ti kəlz) tiny bits of matter that take up space and can be weighed
  Example: The wind blows *particles* of dust through the air.

electromagnetic (i lek′trō mag net′ik) referring to magnetic energy made by a current of electricity
  Example: Electricity can create *electromagnetic* energy.

prism (priz′əm) a clear solid shape that breaks light up into the basic colors
  Example: She held the glass *prism* in a beam of light to see a rainbow of colors.

Academic English

normal (nôr′məl) regular or usual
  Example: The *normal* time to eat breakfast is in the morning.

demonstrate (dem′ən strāt′) to show or explain by using an example
  Example: I will now *demonstrate* how to wrap a present beautifully.

Read again the example sentences that follow the content-area and academic English word definitions. With a partner, discuss the meanings of the words and sentences. Then make up a sentence of your own for each word.

Now skim the article and look for other words that are new to you. Write each new word and its definition in the Personal Dictionary.

While You Read

Tip! **Think about why you read.** Did you know that color comes from light? As you read, try to understand how color depends on light.

Why Is the Ocean Blue?

1 When we say that a banana is yellow or that a leaf is green, we mean that each of those things seems to be that color when we look at it in **normal** light. The color of an object depends on the way it **reflects** and **absorbs** light.

Working with light is very hard for scientists. Light is energy that sometimes
5 moves like waves and sometimes moves like **particles.** When people use the word *light,* they are usually talking about light as **electromagnetic** energy that we can see.

The movement of light does not only help us recognize size and shape, however. It also helps us see colors. If you are awake at dawn, you can notice
10 how colors gradually become clearer as the sky grows brighter.

Light moves in waves when it makes colors. White light—like sunlight—is made up of a mixture of colors. Each color of light has a different wavelength, or distance between waves. When a person shines a stream of white light through a piece of glass called a **prism,** the glass bends the waves in different ways. This
15 makes a rainbow of colors—red, orange, yellow, green, blue, indigo, and violet. This group of colors is known as the spectrum. Red is the color of the spectrum that has the longest wavelength, and violet is the color that has the shortest.

When light reaches an object, some wavelengths of light are absorbed. Others are reflected. An object looks like a certain color because of the color of light it
20 reflects. A leaf looks green because it reflects the green light. An apple looks red because it reflects the red light. Some objects absorb all of the colors of light, and some absorb none. An object that appears black absorbs all of the colors of light. None are reflected. An object that appears white reflects all of the colors of light. None are absorbed.

25 You can **demonstrate** how color depends on light by looking at a red apple in blue light. In this light, the apple does not look red because there is no red light for the apple to reflect. Because the apple's skin absorbs all of the other colors of light, the apple looks black.

A few things, such as glass and water, do not reflect much light. Some
30 wavelengths of light travel through these items, and other wavelengths are absorbed. Green-colored glass, for example, allows green light to pass through it and absorbs all other colors. When sunlight shines on ocean water, something different happens. The light touches tiny particles in the water and is scattered, or reflected in many directions. Blue light, which has the shortest wavelength, is
35 scattered more than other colors. That is the reason that the water often looks blue.

LANGUAGE CONNECTION

Reflects and *absorbs* are antonyms, or opposites. If something reflects light, it causes light to bounce off its surface. If something absorbs light, it pulls light in, the way a sponge draws in moisture.

CONTENT CONNECTION

When you see a *rainbow* in the sky, it is raining in one part of the sky and sunny in another. Raindrops become a *prism* when the sunlight shines through them. That is what causes a rainbow. What other things can act as prisms?

After You Read

A. Organizing Ideas

What causes color? Complete the chart below. Fill in the missing causes and effects.

Causes	→	Effects
Light shines through a prism.		
		Leaves look green.
An object absorbs all light.		
		The object appears white.
Light travels through glass.		Clear glass has no color.
Sunlight hits particles in ocean water, and the light scatters.		

What did you learn about how color is caused? Write two or more sentences about these main ideas. Did the chart help you reach any conclusions? Why or why not?

_____

_____

_____

_____

_____

_____

B. Comprehension Skills

Tip! **Think about how to find answers.** Think about what each sentence means. Try to say it to yourself in your own words before you complete it.

Mark box **a, b,** or **c** with an **X** before the choice that best completes each sentence.

Recalling Facts

1. When a beam of white light passes through a prism, the light is bent to show
   - ☐ **a.** its speed.
   - ☐ **b.** the spectrum.
   - ☐ **c.** its brightness.

2. An object looks like a certain color because of the color of light it
   - ☐ **a.** reflects.
   - ☐ **b.** absorbs.
   - ☐ **c.** produces.

3. An object that absorbs all of the colors of light looks
   - ☐ **a.** blue.
   - ☐ **b.** black.
   - ☐ **c.** white.

4. The ocean looks blue because
   - ☐ **a.** sunlight is yellow.
   - ☐ **b.** water is always blue.
   - ☐ **c.** water scatters blue light.

5. The color of light depends on its
   - ☐ **a.** brightness.
   - ☐ **b.** wavelength.
   - ☐ **c.** number of watts.

Understanding Ideas

1. From the article, you can conclude that a banana looks yellow because it
   - ☐ **a.** absorbs yellow light.
   - ☐ **b.** reflects yellow light.
   - ☐ **c.** absorbs all light.

2. You can also conclude that a certain fruit punch looks red because
   - ☐ **a.** the punch reflects all other colors.
   - ☐ **b.** the punch does not absorb any light.
   - ☐ **c.** the punch scatters red light the most.

3. A black object in sunlight will probably become hotter than a white object because
   - ☐ **a.** light passes through the black object.
   - ☐ **b.** the wavelength of black light is longest.
   - ☐ **c.** black absorbs light, but white reflects it.

4. From the article, you can conclude that the deepest parts of the ocean are dark because, as light passes through so much water,
   - ☐ **a.** none of the light is absorbed.
   - ☐ **b.** only black light is not absorbed.
   - ☐ **c.** all of the colors of light are absorbed.

5. You can also conclude that all color in the world comes from
   - ☐ **a.** light.
   - ☐ **b.** paints.
   - ☐ **c.** pencils.

C. Reading Strategies

1. Recognizing Words in Context

Find the word *mixture* in the article. One definition below is closest to the meaning of that word. One definition has the opposite or nearly the opposite meaning. The remaining definition has a meaning that has nothing to do with the other two words. Label the definitions **C** for *closest,* **O** for *opposite* or *nearly opposite,* and **U** for *unrelated.*

_____ **a.** things that are put together

_____ **b.** things that contain color

_____ **c.** things that are separated

2. Distinguishing Fact from Opinion

Two of the statements below present *facts,* which can be proved. The other statement is an *opinion,* which expresses someone's thoughts or beliefs. Label the statements **F** for *fact* and **O** for *opinion.*

_____ **a.** A leaf looks green because it reflects green light.

_____ **b.** A prism bends light in different ways and makes the spectrum.

_____ **c.** Orange is the most popular color in the spectrum.

3. Making Correct Inferences

Two of the statements below are correct *inferences,* or reasonable guesses, that are based on information in the article. The other statement is an incorrect, or faulty, inference. Label the statements **C** for *correct* inference and **I** for *incorrect* inference.

_____ **a.** A violet shirt looks violet because it reflects violet light.

_____ **b.** A swimming pool would not absorb much light.

_____ **c.** Many colors have the same wavelengths.

4. Understanding Main Ideas

One of the statements below expresses the main idea of the article. Another statement is too general, or too broad. The other explains only part of the article; it is too narrow. Label the statements **M** for *main idea,* **B** for *too broad,* and **N** for *too narrow.*

_____ **a.** Some objects absorb every color of light, and some objects absorb none of the colors.

_____ **b.** When we see the color of an object, we are really seeing the way the object reflects or absorbs light waves.

_____ **c.** When we talk about color, we are actually talking about light.

5. Responding to the Article

Complete the following sentence in your own words:

Before reading "Why Is the Ocean Blue?" I already knew

_____

_____

D. Expanding Vocabulary

Content-Area Words

Cross out one word or phrase in each row that is not related to the word in dark type.

1. **absorbs**	takes in	holds	keeps	releases
2. **reflects**	light	storm	gives back	heat
3. **particles**	water	light	tiny	matter
4. **electromagnetic**	energy	electricity	light	object
5. **prism**	red	black	blue	yellow

Academic English

In the article "Why Is the Ocean Blue?" you learned that *normal* means "regular or usual." *Normal* can also mean "occurring naturally," as in the following sentence.

Warm weather is normal in the summer.

Complete the sentence below.

1. A body temperature of 98.6 degrees Fahrenheit is *normal* for a healthy _____

Now use the word *normal* in a sentence of your own.

2. _____

_____

You also learned that *demonstrate* means "to show or explain by using an example." *Demonstrate* can also mean "to prove or make clear by reasoning or evidence," as in the following sentence.

The flood served to demonstrate the effects of erosion on the land.

Complete the sentence below.

3. A math teacher can *demonstrate* how to solve the geometry _____

Now use the word *demonstrate* in two sentences of your own.

4. _____

5. _____

 Share your new sentences with a partner.

Lesson 14

How Humans Hear

Before You Read

 Think about what you know. Read the lesson title above. What do you predict the article will be about? What do you know about the way your ears work?

Vocabulary

The content-area and academic English words below appear in "How Humans Hear." Read the definitions and the example sentences.

Content-Area Words

vibrates (vī′brāts) moves or shakes back and forth
   Example: The ground *vibrates* during an earthquake.

eardrum (ēr′drum′) a thin layer of skin that separates the parts of the ear and vibrates when sound waves reach it
   Example: Sound waves make the *eardrum* vibrate.

analyzes (an′əl īz′iz) examines or studies in detail
   Example: The detective *analyzes* the clues to find the suspect.

memory (mem′ər ē) the collection, in the mind, of things learned and remembered
   Example: Information is stored in your *memory*.

sensory cortex (sen′sər ē kôr′teks) the part of the brain that relates to the senses
   Example: The *sensory cortex* helps you understand what a sound is.

Academic English

structure (struk′chər) something built or made up of parts
   Example: A school is a large *structure* with different kinds of rooms.

perceives (pər sēvz′) recognizes (something) through one of the senses
   Example: She *perceives*, from the smell of fresh bread, that she is in a bakery.

Do any of the words above seem related? Sort the seven vocabulary words into two or more categories. Write the words down on note cards or in a chart. Words may fit into more than one group. You may wish to work with a partner for this activity. Label one category *Brain*.

Dictionary Now skim the article and look for other words that are new to you. Write each new word and its definition in the Personal Dictionary.

While You Read

Tip! **Think about why you read.** Do you listen to music? Have you ever wondered how your ears hear the different sounds? Write down a question about hearing that you have wondered about. As you read, you may find the answer.

How Humans HEAR

1　Everything that humans hear is in the form of waves. Just as our eyes see light waves as colors, our ears hear sound waves as noises or music. Sound waves are vibrations that move through the air without being seen. The ear and the eye change, or translate, these waves into nerve signals or messages that the brain can 5　understand. The way we hear is made up of several steps.

　　Sound waves are made when something **vibrates** in the air. For example, if you drop a fork on a table, the fork vibrates and creates sound waves. Sound waves reach a part of the ear called the **eardrum.** As the sound hits the eardrum, it causes other things to happen. The eardrum vibrates and moves a group of 10　small bones. The bones are attached to the cochlea, a **structure** that is shaped like a snail's shell. When the small bones move, liquid inside the cochlea moves, too. The liquid covers small hairs called cilia, which move whenever the liquid moves. The cilia are attached to nerve cells that send signals to the brain. The brain **analyzes** these signals to find out what kind of sound they are from.

15　The ears and brain are really good at recognizing or remembering certain sounds. For example, a mother often can tell when her baby is crying even if there are other crying babies in the same room. This is because the sound of her baby's cry has special meaning to her and her brain remembers it.

　　Recognizing sounds takes practice. As the brain receives information 20　about sounds every day, the information is stored in its **memory.** When the brain **perceives** new sounds, it figures out what the new sounds are from the information that is already in the memory. This is why certain words or songs can make a person happy. It may not be the words or songs that make someone feel good. It may be that the sounds remind the person of happy times or things.

25　Another way the brain helps us hear is by figuring out where a sound is coming from. One ear is usually closer to whatever is making a sound than the other ear is. Sound waves are stronger when they reach the ear that is closer. They also reach the closer ear first. A part of the brain called the **sensory cortex** understands these differences and uses them to find out where the sound is 30　coming from.

LANGUAGE CONNECTION

Hit can mean "to touch with force," as in "a bat hits a baseball." *Hit* also means "to reach or touch a place," as in "the sound hits the eardrum." Can you use *hit* this way in a sentence?

CONTENT CONNECTION

Memory is connected to all of our senses. We recall things we did in the places we *see*. The feel of something we *touch* reminds us of other things. The *taste* of certain foods brings past events to mind. Which sense do you think is most connected to memory?

After You Read

A. Organizing Ideas

What is the hearing process? Complete the flowchart below. In each circle, write a step in the process of hearing sounds. Follow the arrows and write the steps in order. Refer to the article to help you. The first and last steps have been done for you.

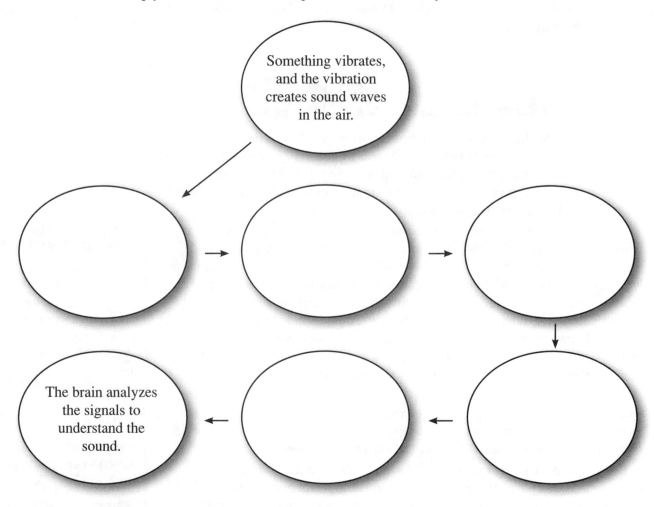

Which parts of the hearing process did you not know about until you read the article? Write two or more sentences about what you did not know before you read the article. Did completing the flowchart help you understand the hearing process? Explain your answer.

_____

_____

_____

_____

_____

B. Comprehension Skills

 Think about how to find answers. Look back at what you read. The information is in the text, but you may have to look in several sentences to find it.

Mark box **a**, **b**, or **c** with an **X** before the choice that best completes each sentence.

Recalling Facts

1. Both sound and light
   - ☐ **a.** move in waves.
   - ☐ **b.** are carried in electrical currents.
   - ☐ **c.** create nerve signals in the cochlea.

2. The cochlea contains
   - ☐ **a.** mostly blood.
   - ☐ **b.** only air.
   - ☐ **c.** liquid.

3. Between the eardrum and the cochlea lies
   - ☐ **a.** a group of small bones.
   - ☐ **b.** a line of cilia.
   - ☐ **c.** empty space.

4. To figure out where a sound is coming from requires the work of the
   - ☐ **a.** brain stem.
   - ☐ **b.** spinal cord.
   - ☐ **c.** sensory cortex.

5. Sound waves are created by
   - ☐ **a.** nerve signals.
   - ☐ **b.** vibrations in the air.
   - ☐ **c.** movements of the eardrum.

Understanding Ideas

1. From the article, you can conclude that a person's response to sound is affected by
   - ☐ **a.** intelligence.
   - ☐ **b.** experiences.
   - ☐ **c.** taste in music.

2. You can also conclude that if eardrums are badly hurt,
   - ☐ **a.** sound will simply bounce off them.
   - ☐ **b.** the sensory cortex will stop working.
   - ☐ **c.** the brain will be unable to identify sounds.

3. The easiest sounds for a brain to recognize are those that
   - ☐ **a.** are the loudest.
   - ☐ **b.** are the most familiar.
   - ☐ **c.** are the most pleasant.

4. A mother can probably recognize her baby's cry in a noisy room because
   - ☐ **a.** her brain tells her that the sound is important.
   - ☐ **b.** she knows that the cry means the baby is sick.
   - ☐ **c.** the cry is much louder than all of the other sounds.

5. From the article, you can conclude that a person who has lost hearing in one ear will find it hard to tell
   - ☐ **a.** the loudness of a sound.
   - ☐ **b.** what is making a sound.
   - ☐ **c.** where a sound is coming from.

C. Reading Strategies

1. Recognizing Words in Context

Find the word *attached* in the article. One definition below is closest to the meaning of that word. One definition has the opposite or nearly the opposite meaning. The remaining definition has a meaning that has nothing to do with the other two words. Label the definitions **C** for *closest*, **O** for *opposite* or *nearly opposite*, and **U** for *unrelated*.

_____ **a.** not connected

_____ **b.** stuck to

_____ **c.** under

2. Distinguishing Fact from Opinion

Two of the statements below present *facts*, which can be proved. The other statement is an *opinion*, which expresses someone's thoughts or beliefs. Label the statements **F** for *fact* and **O** for *opinion*.

_____ **a.** When something vibrates in the air, sound waves are created.

_____ **b.** The brain remembers more happy sounds than sad sounds.

_____ **c.** The sensory cortex helps identify the direction a sound is coming from.

3. Making Correct Inferences

Two of the statements below are correct *inferences,* or reasonable guesses, that are based on information in the article. The other statement is an incorrect, or faulty, inference. Label the statements **C** for *correct* inference and **I** for *incorrect* inference.

_____ **a.** The ears and brain work together to help us hear.

_____ **b.** The brain remembers sounds that have special meaning to us.

_____ **c.** Left ears hear more sounds than right ears.

4. Understanding Main Ideas

One of the statements below expresses the main idea of the article. Another statement is too general, or too broad. The other explains only part of the article; it is too narrow. Label the statements **M** for *main idea,* **B** for *too broad,* and **N** for *too narrow.*

_____ **a.** Without ears, we could not hear.

_____ **b.** Tiny parts within our ears work with our brain to help us hear, remember, and determine where sounds are coming from.

_____ **c.** Sound waves enter the ear and bounce off the eardrum.

5. Responding to the Article

Complete the following sentence in your own words:

Reading "How Humans Hear" made me want to learn more about

_____

_____

D. Expanding Vocabulary

Content-Area Words

Complete each analogy with a word from the box. Write in the missing word.

| vibrates | eardrum | analyzes | memory | sensory cortex |

1. tongue : mouth :: _____ : ear

2. jumps : hops :: _____ : shakes

3. cochlea : ear :: _____ : brain

4. yells : screams :: _____ : studies

5. toolbox : tools :: _____ : information

Academic English

In the article "How Humans Hear," you learned that *structure* is a noun that means "something built or made up of parts." *Structure* can also be a verb meaning "to build or arrange something from parts," as in the following sentence.

Will you structure the art class so that thirty students can paint at the same time?

Complete the sentence below.

1. To *structure* your report well, you should develop a good _____

Now use the word *structure* in a sentence of your own.

2. _____

_____

You also learned that *perceives* means "recognizes (something) through one of the senses." *Perceives* can also mean "recognizes (something) through reason or other means," as in the following sentence.

She perceives that it is time to leave.

Complete the sentence below.

3. A person sometimes *perceives* that he or she is not welcome by using _____

Now use the word *perceives* in two sentences of your own.

4. _____

5. _____

 Share your new sentences with a partner.

Before You Read

 Think about what you know. Read the title and the first two sentences of the article on the opposite page. What do you think the article might be about? What do you know about the ways people from a long time ago counted things?

Vocabulary

The content-area and academic English words below appear in "The History of Numbers." Read the definitions and the example sentences.

Content-Area Words

civilizations (siv'ə li zā'shənz) groups of people living and working together
> *Example:* In history class, we studied the *civilizations* of ancient Egypt and Greece.

tokens (tō'kənz) small objects, such as coins, that are used to count or stand for something
> *Example:* In some cities, you must put *tokens* in a machine to ride on a bus.

pyramids (pir'ə midz') huge stone structures that have four triangle-shaped sides that meet in a point
> *Example:* The Egyptians built large *pyramids* in past ages.

accurate (ak'yər it) having few or no mistakes
> *Example:* His math solutions were always *accurate*.

place value (plās val'ū) the meaning or worth of a number depending on its position
> *Example:* In the number *23,* these are the *place values:* the *2* stands for "two tens," and the *3* stands for "three ones."

Academic English

methods (meth'ədz) ways or systems for reaching a goal
> *Example:* Boiling and frying are *methods* of cooking.

purchase (pur'chəs) to buy
> *Example:* People *purchase* food at a grocery store.

Answer the questions below. Circle the part of each question that is the answer. The first one has been done for you.

1. Would you *purchase* an umbrella for (a rainstorm) or a windstorm?
2. To be *accurate* with words, would you consult a scale or a dictionary?
3. Are *pyramids* more like statues or buildings?
4. Would you call a *civilization* a group of people or a town?
5. Does *place value* make clear the value of sentences or of numbers?
6. For *methods* of cooking, would you look in a recipe book or an encyclopedia?
7. Which would make better *tokens,* small stones or small stores?

 Now skim the article and look for other words that are new to you. Write each new word and its definition in the Personal Dictionary.

While You Read

 Think about why you read. People use numbers every day. How do you use numbers in your daily activities? Do you ever count things in a way other than with numbers?

The History of Numbers

1 People have not always used numbers. It took thousands of years before people started to use number systems, or sets of ideas that explained numbers. In the earliest **civilizations,** people used tallies to keep track of how many items there were of a kind. Tallies are groups of lines or marks that people draw somewhere
5 to count something. Some people marked tallies on sticks or bones. Others counted piles of beads or shells. These simple **methods** for counting worked fine, because people long ago hardly ever had to count large numbers of items.

Scholars who study the history of numbers believe that some people who lived long ago counted by pointing to parts of their bodies. Different parts, such as
10 fingers and elbows, stood for different numbers. Today, people such as the Paiela people of Papua New Guinea still count this way. The largest number used by the Paiela is 28. They use this counting system when they farm or when they **purchase** goods, such as food and supplies.

When the first towns and villages began to appear, people needed better
15 ways to count. The farmers who lived in villages in one ancient, or very old, civilization in the Middle East used different sets of clay **tokens** to count different kinds of things. They used small, flat circles called disks to count sheep, but they used egg-shaped tokens to count jars of oil.

About 5,000 years ago, a new kind of number system appeared. The Sumerians,
20 who lived in what is now the country of Iraq, developed this system soon after they had developed one of the first systems of writing. In the Sumerian number system, the same set of written lines or shapes, called marks, was used to count every kind of thing. The ancient Egyptians, the people of Egypt, used a set of pictures in their system. The Mayan people of Mexico and Central America used a series of written
25 circles and short lines, called dots and dashes.

Number systems helped people do many new things and enjoy an easier life. The Egyptians used numbers to help them measure and build the **pyramids.** Numbers made it easy for them to buy and sell things, to manage their farms, and to tell time. Numbers helped the Maya make one of the first **accurate** calendars.

30 The system of numbers that we use today in most parts of the world began in India about the year 500. This system uses ten numerals, or symbols that stand for a certain number, from *0* to *9*. Their value, or meaning, depends on where they appear in a number. **Place value** lets people quickly solve any math problems that involve addition, subtraction, multiplication, and division with
35 large numbers. New and exciting ideas and inventions have caused us to think of very large and very small numbers. In the last century, the name *googol* was created for a number made up of the number *1* followed by one hundred *0*s.

LANGUAGE CONNECTION

The word *scholar* comes from the same word root as *school*. What other words can you think of that come from the same root?

CONTENT CONNECTION

The Egyptians used math to help them create simple machines. With these they were able to build the huge pyramids. How do you use math to get jobs done?

After You Read

A. Organizing Ideas

How have people counted throughout history? Complete the web below. In each circle, write down an example of a way people have counted things. Refer to the article to help you find answers and add circles if you need them. The first one has been done for you.

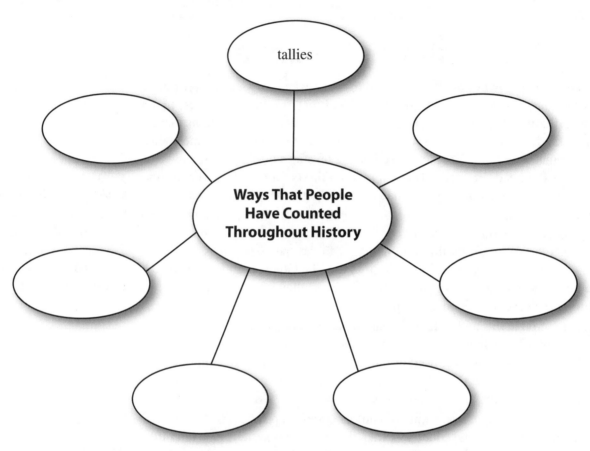

How have new systems of counting helped improve our lives? Write two or more sentences to answer this question. Did filling in the web help you answer this question? Why or why not?

_____

_____

_____

_____

_____

_____

B. Comprehension Skills

Tip! **Think about how to find answers.** Think about what each sentence means. Try to say it to yourself in your own words before you complete it.

Mark box **a**, **b**, or **c** with an **X** before the choice that best completes each sentence.

Recalling Facts

1. To tell how many of an item they had, people in civilizations many years ago used
   - ☐ **a.** clay tablets.
   - ☐ **b.** only the numbers *0–9.*
   - ☐ **c.** tallies.

2. To count, farmers in some of the first villages or cities used
   - ☐ **a.** different kinds of tokens.
   - ☐ **b.** marks on sticks.
   - ☐ **c.** computers.

3. The ancient Sumerians invented a number system that used
   - ☐ **a.** body parts.
   - ☐ **b.** round disks.
   - ☐ **c.** one set of marks to count all things.

4. A number system invented in India about the year 500 is
   - ☐ **a.** no longer used.
   - ☐ **b.** used mainly in India.
   - ☐ **c.** used now in most of the world.

5. The need for large numbers is
   - ☐ **a.** increasing.
   - ☐ **b.** decreasing.
   - ☐ **c.** staying about the same.

Understanding Ideas

1. According to the article, changes in the way we count have been made because
   - ☐ **a.** calculators and computers were invented.
   - ☐ **b.** people's lives have changed.
   - ☐ **c.** people are smarter now.

2. One problem with using tokens to count sheep would be that
   - ☐ **a.** many sheep would run away.
   - ☐ **b.** only 28 tokens can be used.
   - ☐ **c.** large herds of animals would be difficult to count.

3. Compared with the ancient use of numbers, the way we use numbers today has
   - ☐ **a.** led to less buying and selling.
   - ☐ **b.** made it easier to perform calculations.
   - ☐ **c.** made life more difficult.

4. From the article, you can conclude that the ancient Egyptians' number system helped them build the pyramids by allowing them to
   - ☐ **a.** know what kinds of materials they needed.
   - ☐ **b.** invent gasoline-powered equipment.
   - ☐ **c.** use algebra to calculate area.

5. It would be hard to count 100 items in a counting system based on
   - ☐ **a.** body parts.
   - ☐ **b.** picture symbols.
   - ☐ **c.** the numerals *0–9.*

C. Reading Strategies

1. Recognizing Words in Context

Find the word *developed* in the article. One definition below is closest to the meaning of that word. One definition has the opposite or nearly the opposite meaning. The remaining definition has a meaning that has nothing to do with the other two words. Label the definitions **C** for *closest,* **O** for *opposite* or *nearly opposite,* and **U** for *unrelated.*

_____ **a.** destroyed

_____ **b.** varied

_____ **c.** created

2. Distinguishing Fact from Opinion

Two of the statements below present *facts,* which can be proved. The other statement is an *opinion,* which expresses someone's thoughts or beliefs. Label the statements **F** for *fact* and **O** for *opinion.*

_____ **a.** The Sumerians knew more about numbers than the Egyptians did.

_____ **b.** The Mayan people used numbers to make the first working calendar.

_____ **c.** Some people still count using parts of their bodies.

3. Making Correct Inferences

Two of the statements below are correct *inferences,* or reasonable guesses, that are based on information in the article. The other statement is an incorrect, or faulty, inference. Label the statements **C** for *correct* inference and **I** for *incorrect* inference.

_____ **a.** Egyptian picture symbols worked better for counting than tallies.

_____ **b.** The Mayan people used the word *googol* to talk about large numbers.

_____ **c.** Numerals are the numbers *0* through *9.*

4. Understanding Main Ideas

One of the statements below expresses the main idea of the article. Another statement is too general, or too broad. The other explains only part of the article; it is too narrow. Label the statements **M** for *main idea,* **B** for *too broad,* and **N** for *too narrow.*

_____ **a.** The many number systems have now become one basic system that is still changing.

_____ **b.** Through the ages, peoples in many parts of the world have created number systems.

_____ **c.** The Mayan people used dots and dashes as their number system.

5. Responding to the Article

Complete the following sentence in your own words:

What interested me most in "The History of Numbers" was

_____

_____

D. Expanding Vocabulary

Content-Area Words

Complete each sentence with a word from the box. Write the missing word on the line.

pyramids	accurate	civilizations	tokens	place value

1. We call groups of people living together _____.

2. When we play the game, we move _____ around the board.

3. From the window of the airplane, we could see the huge _____.

4. The Mayan civilization made a calendar that was more _____ than any calendar used before it.

5. We are learning about _____ in math class.

Academic English

In the article "The History of Numbers," you learned that *methods* means "ways or systems for reaching a goal." *Methods* can also mean "step-by-step procedures," as in the following sentence.

Among the many methods for finding gold, "panning" was once the most popular.

Complete the sentence below.

1. Sewing, knitting, and crocheting are all *methods* of _____

Now use the word *methods* in a sentence of your own.

2. _____

_____

You also learned that *purchase* is a verb that means "to buy." *Purchase* can also be a noun that means "something that is bought," as in the following sentence.

A car is a costly purchase.

Complete the sentence below.

3. A food *purchase* can be made at a _____

Now use the word *purchase* in two sentences of your own.

4. _____

5. _____

 Share your new sentences with a partner.

Writing a Postcard

Read the postcard. Then complete the sentences. Use words from the Word Bank.

Greetings from Egypt, Isabel!

   This land is beautiful. The (1) _____ here are too dry for most plants, so much of the land is desert. There is so much to learn here! Egypt is one of the oldest (2) _____. Today we saw huge stone buildings called (3) _____. A pyramid is an amazing (4) _____ that took years to build. I am on my way to (5) _____ something special for you!

                        Roman

Word Bank

structure
civilizations
conditions
pyramids
purchase

Isabel Santos
321 Main Street
Hometown
Home State 12345
U.S.A.

Reading an Award Certificate

Read the award certificate. Circle the word that completes each sentence.

Best Science Fair Project

Congratulations, Hector Rodriguez!

Project: Using Your Senses to Help You Remember

In this project, Hector Rodriguez (**analyzes, vibrates**) how people remember things that happened long ago, and he

- creates a model of the brain that shows the (**eardrum, sensory cortex**), the part of the brain that helps people understand the things they see, hear, taste, touch, and smell.

- explains how sensations cause people to recall a (**memory, prism**) from the past.

- explains how the brain (**perceives, tokens**) sensations in a person's environment.

- describes (**particles, methods**) that people can use to help them remember things.

 **Making Connections**

Work with a partner. Talk about what the words mean. How can you use the words to talk about weather? List your ideas in the frame below.

consult	**demonstrate**	**atmosphere**	**moisture**	**humidity**
currents	**normal**	**potentially**	**select**	**attach**

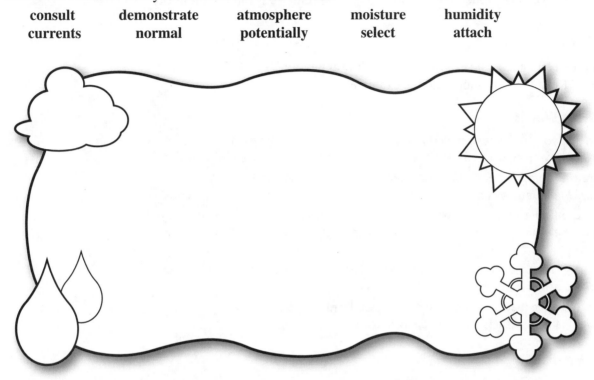

Use all of the words above in complete sentences of your own. Each sentence may include one or more of the words. To help you start writing, look at the ideas you wrote about. After you write your sentences, read them over. If you find a mistake, correct it.

_____

_____

_____

_____

_____

_____

_____

_____

Before You Read

Tip! **Think about what you know.** Read the lesson title above. What do you know about the planet Venus? Have you ever seen Venus in the night sky?

Vocabulary

The content-area and academic English words below appear in "Venus: Earth's Sister Planet." Read the definitions and the example sentences.

Content-Area Words

sulfuric acid (sul fyoor´ik as´id) a powerful, oily chemical that can dissolve many solids
> *Example:* The worker wore special gloves when he used *sulfuric acid* to dissolve metal.

high-pressure (hī´ presh´ər) applying strong force from one thing to another
> *Example: High-pressure* conditions inside Earth can press coal down to form diamonds.

greenhouse (grēn´hous´) a building, made of glass or clear plastic, in which plants are grown
> *Example:* A *greenhouse* keeps the atmosphere warm and humid so that plants inside it can grow.

vapor (vā´pər) a substance, such as smoke or fog, that has turned into a gas that can be seen
> *Example:* Steam is *vapor* that is formed when water is heated.

radar (rā´där) a device that can identify faraway objects by means of sound waves
> *Example:* Planes and ships rely on *radar* to help them stay on course.

Academic English

approximately (ə prok´sə mit lē) nearly or almost
> *Example:* It takes me *approximately* 15 minutes to get to school.

apparent (ə par´ənt) able to be seen
> *Example:* The stars are *apparent* in the sky on a clear night.

Rate each vocabulary word according to the following scale. Write a number next to each content-area and academic English word.

4   I have never seen the word before.

3   I have seen the word but do not know what it means.

2   I know what the word means when I read it.

1   I use the word myself in speaking or writing.

Dictionary Now skim the article and look for other words that are new to you. Write each new word and its definition in the Personal Dictionary.

While You Read

Tip! **Think about why you read.** Have you studied the planets in our solar system? What do you think is the main difference between Earth and other planets, such as Venus? As you read, look for this difference and others.

Venus
Earth's Sister Planet

1   For many reasons, Venus is often called Earth's sister planet. Most of the time, Venus is the planet that is closest to Earth. Venus and Earth are **approximately** the same size. On both Earth and Venus, explosions, or eruptions, of hot melted rock from volcanoes have formed a rocky layer that is much
5   younger than the rest of the planet.

Thick clouds hide the surface, or top layer, of Venus. Some clouds are made of carbon dioxide gas, which is the waste gas we release when we breathe out. Other clouds are made of **sulfuric acid.** Only within the last twenty years have scientists been able to see beneath these clouds with telescopes. We now know that Venus
10   and Earth are alike in some ways but are also very different. Earth's atmosphere, or the air that surrounds the planet, supports life. On Venus the temperature is about 460 degrees Celsius (860 degrees Fahrenheit). This is even hotter than on Mercury, the only planet closer to the Sun than Venus is. Venus is so hot because its thick, **high-pressure** atmosphere holds the Sun's heat in. This trapping of heat
15   is called "the **greenhouse** effect." Scientists believe that Venus once had as much water as Earth. The water got so hot that it boiled. It then turned into water **vapor**.

Like Earth, Venus rotates, or turns—but from east to west. Earth (and most other planets) turn from west to east. Venus rotates slowly: it takes Venus 243 Earth days to make one complete rotation. However, it takes only 225 Earth days
20   for Venus to make one trip around the Sun. This is because Venus is closer to the Sun than Earth is. Venus's orbit, or its path around the Sun, is shaped almost like a circle. Earth's is more elliptical, or oval shaped. Unlike Earth, Venus has no moon.

In 1962 *Mariner 2* became the first spaceship to fly by Venus. This U.S. spaceship was able to tell us how fast the planet rotates. The Soviet Union landed
25   several spaceships on Venus during the 1970s and 1980s. They sent back pictures of the planet's surface. *Magellan,* another U.S. spaceship, used **radar** to draw a map of most of the surface in 1989 and 1990. The photos and maps show that Venus is covered with many hills and large, flat areas called plains.

Except for the Sun and the Moon, Venus is the brightest object in space that
30   is **apparent** from Earth. At times, it can be one of the first objects we see in the night sky as the Sun sets at twilight. At other times, it can be one of the last to disappear, or become hard to see, at sunrise. This is why Venus has been called both the morning star and the evening star.

CONTENT CONNECTION

Celsius and Fahrenheit are temperature scales. In the United States, the Fahrenheit system is more commonly used. How can you tell whether a temperature given is Celsius or Fahrenheit?

LANGUAGE CONNECTION

The suffix *-est* at the end of an adjective means "most." What word would mean "the most old"? "The most happy"?

After You Read

A. Organizing Ideas

How can we compare Earth and Venus? Complete the Venn diagram below. In the outer part of the first circle, list features of Earth. In the outer part of the second circle, list features of Venus. Where the circles overlap, list features that the planets share. Some have been done for you.

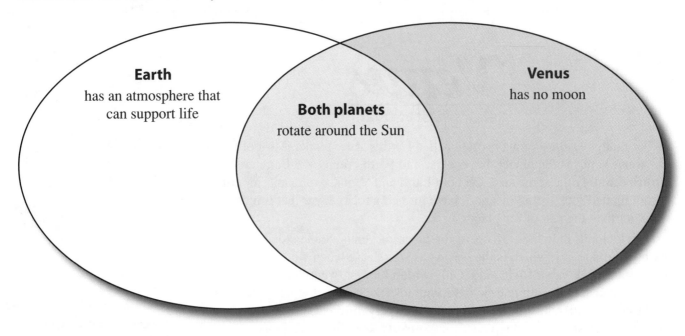

Earth
has an atmosphere that
can support life

Both planets
rotate around the Sun

Venus
has no moon

Do you think that Earth and Venus are very different or not so different? Write two or more sentences to explain your answer. Did the Venn diagram help you answer this question? If so, how?

_____

_____

_____

_____

_____

_____

_____

_____

_____

B. Comprehension Skills

Tip! **Think about how to find answers.** Think about what each sentence means. Try to say it to yourself in your own words before you complete it.

Mark box **a, b,** or **c** with an **X** before the choice that best completes each sentence.

Recalling Facts

1. Venus is
   - ☐ **a.** about the same size as Earth.
   - ☐ **b.** much larger than Earth.
   - ☐ **c.** much smaller than Earth.

2. Venus rotates
   - ☐ **a.** at the same speed as Earth.
   - ☐ **b.** much faster than Earth.
   - ☐ **c.** much more slowly than Earth.

3. Venus is very hot because
   - ☐ **a.** its thick atmosphere traps the Sun's heat.
   - ☐ **b.** it is the closest planet to the Sun.
   - ☐ **c.** it has no clouds to block sunlight.

4. One of the main things found in Venus's atmosphere is
   - ☐ **a.** water vapor.
   - ☐ **b.** oxygen gas.
   - ☐ **c.** carbon dioxide gas.

5. Venus has
   - ☐ **a.** no moon.
   - ☐ **b.** one moon.
   - ☐ **c.** three moons.

Understanding Ideas

1. From the article, you can conclude that Venus and Earth are
   - ☐ **a.** more different than they are alike.
   - ☐ **b.** alike in almost every way.
   - ☐ **c.** not alike at all.

2. You can also conclude that Venus is the
   - ☐ **a.** second closest planet to the Sun.
   - ☐ **b.** third closest planet to the Sun.
   - ☐ **c.** closest planet to the Sun.

3. The main reason it would be hard for astronauts to walk on Venus is that
   - ☐ **a.** there is no water.
   - ☐ **b.** there is not enough oxygen in the atmosphere.
   - ☐ **c.** there are high temperatures and high pressures.

4. Scientists did not know which minerals are on the surface of Venus until
   - ☐ **a.** they had telescopes strong enough to see the surface.
   - ☐ **b.** a Soviet spaceship landed on Venus.
   - ☐ **c.** the *Mariner 2* spaceship flew by Venus.

5. The material on the surface of Venus probably comes from
   - ☐ **a.** meteorites.
   - ☐ **b.** lava.
   - ☐ **c.** sulfuric acid.

C. Reading Strategies

1. Recognizing Words in Context

Find the word *alike* in the article. One definition below is closest to the meaning of that word. One definition has the opposite or nearly the opposite meaning. The remaining definition has a meaning that has nothing to do with the other two words. Label the definitions **C** for *closest*, **O** for *opposite* or *nearly opposite*, and **U** for *unrelated*.

_____ **a.** the same

_____ **b.** alone

_____ **c.** different

2. Distinguishing Fact from Opinion

Two of the statements below present *facts*, which can be proved. The other statement is an *opinion*, which expresses someone's thoughts or beliefs. Label the statements **F** for *fact* and **O** for *opinion*.

_____ **a.** Venus is hot because its atmosphere holds in the heat of the Sun.

_____ **b.** The surface of Venus has many hills and plains.

_____ **c.** It is unsafe for spaceships to study planets like Venus.

3. Making Correct Inferences

Two of the statements below are correct *inferences*, or reasonable guesses, that are based on information in the article. The other statement is an incorrect, or faulty, inference. Label the statements **C** for *correct* inference and **I** for *incorrect* inference.

_____ **a.** It would not be possible for humans or animals to live on Venus.

_____ **b.** If Earth became as hot as Venus, our water would boil and disappear.

_____ **c.** Sometimes when we think we see the Moon at night, we actually see Venus.

4. Understanding Main Ideas

One of the statements below expresses the main idea of the article. Another statement is too general, or too broad. The other explains only part of the article; it is too narrow. Label the statements **M** for *main idea*, **B** for *too broad*, and **N** for *too narrow*.

_____ **a.** Venus has an almost perfectly circular orbit.

_____ **b.** Venus and Earth are alike and also different.

_____ **c.** Even though Venus and Earth are known as sister planets, they have many differences.

5. Responding to the Article

Complete the following sentence in your own words:

From reading "Venus: Earth's Sister Planet," I have learned

_____

_____

D. Expanding Vocabulary

Content-Area Words

Cross out one word or phrase in each row that is not related to the word in dark type.

1. sulfuric acid	rocks	Venus	thick	dangerous
2. high-pressure	weak	strong	forces	atmosphere
3. greenhouse	trap	Moon	heat	Sun
4. vapor	gas	visible	boiled	planet
5. radar	machine	waves	light	bounce

Academic English

In the article "Venus: Earth's Sister Planet," you learned that *approximately* means "nearly or almost." *Approximately* can be used to compare the nearly equal sizes of Venus and Earth. *Approximately* can also be used to compare other things, as in the following sentence.

I need approximately eight hours of sleep each night.

Complete the sentence below.

1. The time of day I get up each morning is *approximately* _____

Now use the word *approximately* in a sentence of your own.

2. _____

_____

You also learned that *apparent* means "able to be seen." *Apparent* can also mean "that seems to be true," as in the following sentence.

The heavy rain has made it apparent that I need to carry an umbrella.

Complete the sentence below.

3. It is *apparent* that you need a drink of water when you feel _____

Now use the word *apparent* in two sentences of your own.

4. _____

5. _____

 Share your new sentences with a partner.

What Is a Reptile?

Before You Read

 Think about what you know. Read the lesson title above. Can you answer the question? What do you already know about reptiles?

Vocabulary

The content-area and academic English words below appear in "What Is a Reptile?" Read the definitions and the example sentences.

Content-Area Words

backbones (bak′bōnz′) the bones that protect the spinal cords and support the bodies of animals and people
> *Example:* *Backbones* protect the nerves in the spinal cord.

venom (ven′əm) something passed on by certain animals through a bite, causing injury or death
> *Example:* The *venom* of bees can kill some people.

prey (prā) an animal that is hunted or killed for food
> *Example:* Mice are *prey* for some birds, and birds are *prey* for cats.

relatives (rel′ə tivs) animals or people that come from the same family
> *Example:* I have many *relatives,* such as aunts, uncles, and cousins.

dinosaurs (dī′nə sôrs′) huge reptiles that lived and died out many ages ago
> *Example:* Scientists study the bones of *dinosaurs.*

Academic English

external (iks turn′əl) located on the outside
> *Example:* Skin is the *external* covering of the body.

capable (kā′pə bəl) having the ability or skill to do something
> *Example:* Cheetahs are *capable* of running very fast.

Read again the example sentences that follow the content-area and academic English word definitions. With a partner, discuss the meanings of the words and sentences. Then make up a sentence of your own for each word.

Dictionary Now skim the article and look for other words that are new to you. Write each new word and its definition in the Personal Dictionary.

While You Read

Tip! **Think about why you read.** There are many kinds of reptiles. How many kinds of reptiles can you name? As you read, look for information about the different reptiles.

What Is a REPTILE?

1 Reptiles are cold-blooded animals that have **backbones.** The word *cold-blooded* refers to animals whose body temperatures change when their **external** environment does. Reptiles have lungs that breathe air, and their bodies are covered with tough scales, or stiff, flat plates. Many are able to go without 5 food for days. Most reptiles hatch, or come from eggs. Some different kinds of reptiles are snakes, lizards, turtles, and crocodilians.

Snakes are the largest group of reptiles. There are more than 3,000 kinds. Their long bodies look like ropes covered with scales. They have no legs, so snakes move by twisting and turning along on the ground or by stretching themselves 10 between tree branches. Snakes may have sharp teeth. Some even have special hollow teeth, or fangs, that are filled with dangerous liquid poison called **venom.** Some snakes swallow their **prey** whole and later spit out the animal parts their bodies cannot use. One large snake, the reticulated python, is **capable** of eating animals that weigh as much as 70 kilograms (154 pounds).

15 Lizards are the next largest group of reptiles. There are more than 2,700 kinds of lizards. Most lizards have four legs and a tail, but some have only two legs or none at all, so they look like snakes. Most lizards have sharp nails called claws, but the gecko has sticky pads on its toes that allow it to climb smooth objects. Almost all lizards eat insects. A few also eat other animals or plants.

20 Turtles are reptiles with hard shells that protect their bodies. They are toothless, but many have sharp-edged beaks. When they are scared or in danger, many turtles pull their heads and limbs, or front and back legs, into their shells. Most turtles live in wet, grassy places called marshes and swamps, or in other bodies of fresh water. Others live in the ocean or on land. Turtles may eat 25 plants, small animals, or both. Many turtles like to eat insects and worms. One small turtle, the box turtle, grows only to about 15 centimeters (6 inches) long. Leatherback sea turtles may grow up to 3.7 meters (12 feet) long. Some kinds of turtles live longer than any other animals, including humans.

The crocodilians are a group of reptiles that includes alligators and crocodiles. 30 They are the largest reptiles and are distant **relatives** of birds. Crocodilians are also believed to be relatives of the **dinosaurs.** Crocodilians live in water and swim by moving their long tails back and forth. They eat birds, fish, and other animals. They grab their prey in their strong jaws, and crush or smash it or swallow it whole. Crocodilians can move on land by crawling or walking on their short legs. 35 Crocodiles have narrow heads that are thinner and more pointed than alligators' heads. Crocodiles usually live in salt water, but alligators live in fresh water.

LANGUAGE CONNECTION

Breathe is a verb that means "to take air in and send it out of the lungs." *Breath* is a noun that means "air that comes in and out during breathing." One way to remember which is which is to see that the verb has an *e* at the end of it.

CONTENT CONNECTION

Only about 400 kinds of snakes in the world have poisonous bites. The coral snake is poisonous, but the garter snake is not. Can you name another type of poisonous snake?

After You Read

A. Organizing Ideas

What are some kinds of reptiles? Complete the chart below. Label each box with the name of one kind of reptile that the article describes. Under each label, list four important facts about that kind of reptile. Refer to the article to help you. Some boxes have been done for you.

Lizards

- Some have no legs.
- Most have sharp claws.
- _____
- _____
- _____
- _____

_____

- They are protected by a hard shell.
- They may eat plants, small animals, or both.
- _____
- _____
- _____
- _____

_____

- They have long, round bodies covered with scales.
- They have no legs, so they move by twisting along the ground.
- _____
- _____
- _____

Crocodilians

- _____
- _____
- _____
- _____
- _____
- _____

What new information did you learn about reptiles? Write two or more sentences about what you learned. Did the chart help you learn this new information?

_____

_____

_____

_____

_____

B. Comprehension Skills

 Think about how to find answers. Look back at what you read. The information is in the text, but you may have to look in several sentences to find it.

Mark box **a, b,** or **c** with an **X** before the choice that best completes each sentence.

Recalling Facts

1. The largest group of reptiles is made up of
   - ☐ **a.** crocodilians.
   - ☐ **b.** lizards.
   - ☐ **c.** snakes.

2. Crocodilians are distantly related to
   - ☐ **a.** sharks.
   - ☐ **b.** worms.
   - ☐ **c.** birds.

3. Most reptiles
   - ☐ **a.** hatch from eggs.
   - ☐ **b.** are fed milk by their mothers after they are born.
   - ☐ **c.** ride on their mothers' backs when they are young.

4. The reptiles that live the longest are
   - ☐ **a.** turtles.
   - ☐ **b.** crocodilians.
   - ☐ **c.** lizards.

5. The largest reptiles are
   - ☐ **a.** pythons.
   - ☐ **b.** leatherback sea turtles.
   - ☐ **c.** crocodilians.

Understanding Ideas

1. From this article, you can conclude that
   - ☐ **a.** reptiles look very different, but they all have tails.
   - ☐ **b.** all reptiles look alike and act alike.
   - ☐ **c.** reptiles can look different, but they are alike in other important ways.

2. You can also conclude that turtles
   - ☐ **a.** are cold-blooded.
   - ☐ **b.** can breathe while under water.
   - ☐ **c.** spend most of their time on land.

3. Fish lay eggs and have scales, but they are not like any reptiles because they
   - ☐ **a.** live only in the water.
   - ☐ **b.** have no legs.
   - ☐ **c.** do not have lungs for breathing air.

4. A lizard would probably eat a
   - ☐ **a.** peanut.
   - ☐ **b.** beetle.
   - ☐ **c.** mouse.

5. It is not likely that you would find a reptile near a
   - ☐ **a.** desert.
   - ☐ **b.** swamp.
   - ☐ **c.** volcano.

C. Reading Strategies

1. Recognizing Words in Context

Find the word *protect* in the article. One definition below is closest to the meaning of that word. One definition has the opposite or nearly the opposite meaning. The remaining definition has a meaning that has nothing to do with the other two words. Label the definitions **C** for *closest*, **O** for *opposite* or *nearly opposite*, and **U** for *unrelated*.

_____ **a.** get dirty

_____ **b.** keep safe

_____ **c.** put in danger

2. Distinguishing Fact from Opinion

Two of the statements below present *facts*, which can be proved. The other statement is an *opinion*, which expresses someone's thoughts or beliefs. Label the statements **F** for *fact* and **O** for *opinion*.

_____ **a.** Turtles have no teeth.

_____ **b.** Reptiles are uglier than mammals.

_____ **c.** Some snakes have poisonous fangs.

3. Making Correct Inferences

Two of the statements below are correct *inferences*, or reasonable guesses, that are based on information in the article. The other statement is an incorrect, or faulty, inference. Label the statements **C** for *correct* inference and **I** for *incorrect* inference.

_____ **a.** Reptiles such as pythons could probably eat a dog.

_____ **b.** Some reptiles that look like snakes may actually be lizards.

_____ **c.** There are more lizards than any other kind of reptile.

4. Understanding Main Ideas

One of the statements below expresses the main idea of the article. Another statement is too general, or too broad. The other explains only part of the article; it is too narrow. Label the statements **M** for *main idea*, **B** for *too broad*, and **N** for *too narrow*.

_____ **a.** Although they live in different places and have different sizes and shapes, all reptiles share certain characteristics.

_____ **b.** Many people think that crocodilians are related to birds and dinosaurs.

_____ **c.** Reptiles are cold-blooded animals that have backbones.

5. Responding to the Article

Complete the following sentences in your own words:

One of the things I practiced best while reading "What Is a Reptile?" was

_____

I think that I did this well because _____

_____

D. Expanding Vocabulary

Content-Area Words

Complete each sentence with a word from the box. Write the missing word on the line.

prey	backbones	dinosaurs	venom	relatives

1. Like humans, reptiles have_____to support their bodies.

2. The hollow fangs of some snakes contain dangerous_____ .

3. Some snakes swallow their _____ without chewing it.

4. Crocodilians are _____of birds and dinosaurs.

5. The largest reptiles that have ever lived are called_____.

Academic English

In the article "What Is a Reptile?" you learned that *external* is an adjective that means "located on the outside." *External* can also be an noun that means "something outside the main part," as in the following sentence.

  "Beauty is merely an external," her mother said.

Complete the sentence below.

1. Music was considered an *external* in school, not part of the regular _____

Now use the word *external* in a sentence of your own.

2. _____

_____

You also learned that *capable* means "having the ability or skill to do something." *Capable* can also mean "having traits leaning toward something," as in the following sentence.

  Some psychologists believe that all people are capable of committing crimes.

Complete the sentence below.

3. Hurricanes and tornadoes are storms that are *capable* of causing great _____

Now use the word *capable* in two sentences of your own.

4. _____

5. _____

 Share your new sentences with a partner.

The Parts of a Flowering Plant

Before You Read

Tip! **Think about what you know.** Read the lesson title above. What do you predict the article will be about? What parts of plants and flowers do you already know?

Vocabulary

The content-area and academic English words below appear in "The Parts of a Flowering Plant." Read the definitions and the example sentences.

Content-Area Words

carpel (kär′pəl) the part of the plant that contains the seeds
> *Example:* When the pollen entered the *carpel,* seeds began to grow.

pollen (pol′ən) the powdery material that makes seeds develop
> *Example:* The yellow dust on my fingers was *pollen* from the flowers I picked.

pollination (pol′ə nā′shən) the process by which pollen is transferred to the carpel of a flower
> *Example:* The process of *pollination* is helped by bees and other insects.

attract (ə trakt′) to make something come closer because of interest or feeling
> *Example:* Lights may *attract* insects such as moths.

photosynthesis (fō′tə sin′thə sis) a process through which plant cells use sunlight to make food for the plant
> *Example:* The process of *photosynthesis* causes plants to be green.

Academic English

job (job) work that is supposed to be done
> *Example:* For some animals, it is the *job* of both parents to feed their young.

secure (si kyoor′) kept or held firmly
> *Example:* People make their homes *secure* by locking their doors.

Complete the sentences below that contain the content-area and academic English words above. Use the spaces provided. The first one has been done for you.

1. The *carpel,* deep inside a blossom, produces seeds_____.
2. *Photosynthesis* is the process plants use to _____.
3. Water in the desert will *attract* _____.
4. The *job* of a student is _____.
5. A bank must be made *secure* because _____.
6. *Pollination* is the process of transferring pollen to a _____.
7. *Pollen* from the stamens is carried from flower to flower by
   wind and _____.

Dictionary Now skim the article and look for other words that are new to you. Write each new word and its definition in the Personal Dictionary.

While You Read

Tip! **Think about why you read.** Each part of a plant has a job that helps the plant live. Do you grow plants inside your home or in a garden? As you read, think about plants you have seen. Try to remember the different parts.

The Parts of a Flowering Plant

1 Plants that grow flowers are called angiosperms. About 80 percent (or eight out of ten) of all green plants are angiosperms. Parts of angiosperms are eaten by many animals that live on land. These plants also give us medicine, paper, hardwood, and other useful things. Flowering plants have four main parts: flowers, 5 leaves, stems, and roots. Each part has an important job.

Flowers come in many colors, shapes, and sizes. The **job** of the flower is to make seeds that can grow into new plants. Seeds are formed in the middle of a flower, in the **carpel** (some plants have more than one). Next to the carpel are the stamens. These are thin plant parts that produce pollen. For seeds to grow, 10 **pollen** from the stamens must enter the carpels. This process is called **pollination.** Pollination takes place when the wind, birds, or insects move pollen from stamen to carpel inside the same plant or from plant to plant. It is usually better for a flower to get pollen from a different plant. Around the stamens are the petals. Petals give flowers their color and smell. The color and smell help **attract** insects 15 and birds to the plants, which helps pollination take place.

Leaves come in many shapes and sizes. They make food for angiosperms through a process called **photosynthesis.** Inside leaves are tiny cells called chloroplasts, which are filled with a green chemical called chlorophyll. The chloroplasts take in energy from sunlight and turn it into food energy for the plant. 20 Leaves have tiny holes called stomata that allow gases such as carbon dioxide to come in and gases such as oxygen to get out. If a plant takes in too much water, the plant can push it out through the stomata.

Stems hold up the leaves and flowers. They also carry food and water to other parts of the plant. Stems have small bumps, called buds, growing on their sides. 25 Buds turn into leaves and flowers. In some plants, large buds called bulbs grow under the ground and hold food that feeds a plant through the winter. Tulips and daffodils are examples of flowering plants that have bulbs. The stems of flowering trees are made of wood and are called trunks.

A plant's roots keep the plant **secure** in the dirt. They also take in the water 30 and tiny pieces of minerals that the plant needs to live. Almost all roots grow underground. Some angiosperms have a taproot, which is a thick main root that grows downward and has smaller roots branching from it. Others have fibrous roots. Fibrous roots are thinner and spread out closer to the surface than taproots do. These tiny hairlike roots also take in more water and minerals.

CONTENT CONNECTION

The carpel is a seed pod formed when the petals of a blossom dry up and fall off a plant. Trees produce fruit in the same way. Can you think of fruits that have seeds?

LANGUAGE CONNECTION

The suffix -ward means "in the direction of." What does downward mean?

After You Read

A. Organizing Ideas

What are the parts of a flowering plant? Use the space provided to draw a diagram of the four main parts of a flowering plant. Label the parts and write a definition for each one. Make your drawing as detailed as you can.

What did you learn from drawing the diagram about how flowering plants work? Are flowering plants more complex living things than you thought they were? Write two or more sentences about what you learned. How did the diagram help you answer these questions?

_____

_____

_____

_____

_____

B. Comprehension Skills

 Think about how to find answers. Look back at different parts of the text. What facts help you figure out how to complete the sentences?

Mark box **a, b,** or **c** with an **X** before the choice that best completes each sentence.

Recalling Facts

1. The four most important parts of flowering plants are
- ☐ **a.** flowers, leaves, stems, and roots.
- ☐ **b.** flowers, leaves, buds, and petals.
- ☐ **c.** flowers, stems, sepals, and carpels.

2. Flowering plants are also called
- ☐ **a.** angioplasties.
- ☐ **b.** gymnosperms.
- ☐ **c.** angiosperms.

3. The job of a flower is to
- ☐ **a.** protect the plant from being eaten.
- ☐ **b.** support the plant.
- ☐ **c.** produce seeds.

4. Stems
- ☐ **a.** make food for plants.
- ☐ **b.** carry food and water.
- ☐ **c.** keep the plant in one place.

5. A taproot is
- ☐ **a.** a main root that grows downward.
- ☐ **b.** thin and threadlike.
- ☐ **c.** a bulb.

Understanding Ideas

1. From the article, you can conclude that
- ☐ **a.** the flower is the most important part of a flowering plant.
- ☐ **b.** the stem is not so important as the other parts of a plant.
- ☐ **c.** all parts of the plant work together to help the plant survive.

2. You can also conclude that
- ☐ **a.** pollen can travel from flower to flower in several ways.
- ☐ **b.** pollination could never take place without wind.
- ☐ **c.** only insects can pollinate flowers.

3. If a flowering plant had no chloroplasts, the plant would probably
- ☐ **a.** not be able to take in any water.
- ☐ **b.** immediately dry up and die.
- ☐ **c.** not be able to make its own food.

4. Trees can probably survive without leaves in winter because
- ☐ **a.** photosynthesis also takes place in the roots.
- ☐ **b.** trees store food during the seasons in which they have leaves.
- ☐ **c.** trees hibernate, or sleep, during the winter.

5. If you put a potted flowering plant in a dark cupboard, it would probably die because
- ☐ **a.** the roots could not grow.
- ☐ **b.** photosynthesis could not take place.
- ☐ **c.** there would be no insects or wind to spread pollen.

C. Reading Strategies

1. Recognizing Words in Context

Find the word *enter* in the article. One definition below is closest to the meaning of that word. One definition has the opposite or nearly the opposite meaning. The remaining definition has a meaning that has nothing to do with the other two words. Label the definitions **C** for *closest,* **O** for *opposite* or *nearly opposite,* and **U** for *unrelated.*

_____ **a.** go into

_____ **b.** go out

_____ **c.** walk quickly

2. Distinguishing Fact from Opinion

Two of the statements below present *facts,* which can be proved. The other statement is an *opinion,* which expresses someone's thoughts or beliefs. Label the statements **F** for *fact* and **O** for *opinion.*

_____ **a.** Birds, insects, and wind help pollination occur.

_____ **b.** Stomata let water and gases in and out of a plant.

_____ **c.** Roots look like snakes or worms.

3. Making Correct Inferences

Two of the statements below are correct *inferences,* or reasonable guesses, that are based on information in the article. The other statement is an incorrect, or faulty, inference. Label the statements **C** for *correct* inference and **I** for *incorrect* inference.

_____ **a.** Tulips and daffodils could not survive without bulbs.

_____ **b.** Plants that have bulbs do not need roots.

_____ **c.** Without angiosperms, many animals would not have food to eat.

4. Understanding Main Ideas

One of the statements below expresses the main idea of the article. Another statement is too general, or too broad. The other explains only part of the article; it is too narrow. Label the statements **M** for *main idea,* **B** for *too broad,* and **N** for *too narrow.*

_____ **a.** Angiosperms have many parts.

_____ **b.** Leaf cells contain chloroplasts.

_____ **c.** Angiosperms have flowers, leaves, stems, and roots; each part has its own important job.

5. Responding to the Article

Complete the following sentence in your own words:

One thing in "The Parts of a Flowering Plant" that I cannot understand is

_____

_____

D. Expanding Vocabulary

Content-Area Words

Read each item carefully. Write on the line the word or phrase that best completes each sentence.

1. The bright color and the _____ of a flower attract insects.
   feel   taste   smell

2. During photosynthesis, plants use energy from the _____.
   Sun   sky   Moon

3. Insects, birds, and wind can help _____ to occur.
   pollination   carpels   photosynthesis

4. A plant's _____ are found inside the carpel.
   petals   roots   seeds

5. The stamen is the part of the plant that produces _____.
   carbon dioxide   pollen   buds

Academic English

In the article "The Parts of a Flowering Plant," you learned that *job* means "work that is supposed to be done." *Job* can also mean "the work a person is paid to do," as in the following sentence.

Going to college can help you get a good job.

Complete the sentence below.

1. Someone who wants a *job* as a football coach must be good at _____

Now use the word *job* in a sentence of your own.

2. _____

_____

You also learned that *secure* means "kept or held firmly." *Secure* can also mean "safe," as in the following sentence.

Locking your doors at home will help keep you secure.

Complete the sentence below.

3. Wearing a seatbelt and driving carefully are ways to make you *secure* in a _____

Now use the word *secure* in two sentences of your own.

4. _____

5. _____

 Share your new sentences with a partner.

Before You Read

 Think about what you know. Read the first paragraph of the article on the opposite page. Have you ever studied the forces of gravity and air resistance? Read the article to find out more.

Vocabulary

The content-area and academic English words below appear in "Gravity and Air Resistance." Read the definitions and the example sentences.

Content-Area Words

gravity (grav′ə tē) the force that pulls objects toward the ground
Example: *Gravity* caused the book that I dropped to fall to the floor.

resistance (ri zis′təns) an opposing force or power
Example: The *resistance* of the wind fought gravity and kept the feather in the air.

speed (spēd) quickness of movement
Example: Cars move with great *speed* on highways and interstate roads.

surface (sur′fis) the outside or top layer
Example: The *surface* of the bookcase was smooth and shiny.

parachute (par′ə sho͞ot′) an umbrella-like device used to slow down something that is falling through the air and help it land safely on the ground
Example: People who jump from airplanes use a *parachute* to land safely.

Academic English

interact (in′tə rakt′) to work together with or communicate between
Example: Students can *interact* by talking with each other.

utilizes (ū′tə līz′ez) makes use of something
Example: A student *utilizes* a computer to research information.

Answer the questions below. Circle the part of each question that is the answer. The first one has been done for you.

1. Will air *resistance* be seen more (in falling leaves) or in falling apples?
2. A firefighter *utilizes* which of the following tools, a water hose or a screwdriver?
3. Does a *parachute* work by filling up with air or filling up with water?
4. Does a telephone help people *interact* by letting them write or letting them talk?
5. Which moves with greater *speed*, a rabbit or a snail?
6. Which part of a car touches the *surface* of the road, the trunk or the tires?
7. Is *gravity* noticed more when someone drops a ball or when someone holds a ball?

 Now skim the article and look for other words that are new to you. Write each new word and its definition in the Personal Dictionary.

While You Read

 Think about why you read. Have you ever wondered why things on Earth do not float off into space? As you read, try to find the answer.

Gravity and Air Resistance

1 What happens to a baseball that is thrown through the air and to a leaf that is blown from a tree are two examples of how Earth's own forces act on objects in the air. When we release, or let go of, an object in the air, it usually falls down to the ground. To understand what happens to an object in the air, you need
5 to understand **gravity** and air **resistance.** We can think of gravity on Earth as a force pulling us down. Air resistance is an upward force on a falling object. These two forces **interact** to make an object fall at a certain **speed,** or velocity.

Gravity, one of the simplest forces of nature, makes objects fall. Gravity is the force that pulls objects toward Earth. If a person lets go of two objects that are the
10 same size, shape, and weight, they fall at the same speed.

Many people think of air as being weightless, or having no weight. However, air is actually a blend of gases—mostly nitrogen and oxygen—that press on everything that they surround. Earth's atmosphere contains a huge amount of air. Air resistance is the force of the air pushing against a moving object. Air
15 resistance is also called drag. The amount of air resistance an object meets when it falls depends mostly on its weight, shape, and size. For example, think about a 6-kilogram (13-pound) flat piece of plastic and a 6-kilogram bowling ball being dropped from the top of a tall building at the same time. The bowling ball would hit the ground much sooner than the piece of plastic would. The reason is that the
20 plastic would meet more air resistance on its way down. This is mostly because the flat piece of plastic has a much larger **surface** than the bowling ball has. More air would be pushing against the plastic than would be pushing against the bowling ball.

If two objects have the same shape and weight but different sizes, the smaller
25 object will usually fall faster. Imagine a 6-kilogram ball made of plastic that is larger than another 6-kilogram ball made of metal. More air will push on the larger object, so the metal ball will fall faster.

A **parachute utilizes** air resistance to slow a person's fall. Even though a person weighs more with a parachute than without one, the parachute still helps
30 the person to fall more slowly to the ground. An open parachute creates a large surface area and meets with more air resistance.

LANGUAGE CONNECTION

Let go is a verb phrase that means "to release something." If you let go of an object, gravity will cause it to fall. What would happen if you let go of something in a place where there was no gravity?

CONTENT CONNECTION

A sheet of paper has more surface than depth, so it meets great air resistance. Decreasing an object's air resistance makes it fall faster. How would you make a sheet of paper dropped from the top of a building reach the ground faster?

After You Read

A. Organizing Ideas

What are gravity and air resistance? Complete the outline below for the article. For each paragraph, write the topic on the first line and at least two facts about that topic on the lines below it. Refer to the article to help you. Some have been done for you.

Paragraph 1: Gravity and air resistance work together on objects.

1. _____

2. _____

Paragraph 2: _____

1. _____

2. Gravity pulls objects toward Earth.

3. _____

Paragraph 3: _____

1. _____

2. _____

3. Objects with a larger surface meet with more air resistance.

Paragraph 4: _____

1. _____

2. _____

3. _____

Paragraph 5: _____

1. A parachute uses air resistance to make something fall more slowly.

2. _____

3. _____

What did you learn about how gravity and air resistance work together? Write two or more sentences about what you learned. How did the outline help you understand the article?

_____

_____

B. Comprehension Skills

Tip! **Think about how to find answers.** Think about what each sentence means. Try to say it to yourself in your own words before you complete it.

Mark box **a, b,** or **c** with an **X** before the choice that best completes each sentence.

Recalling Facts

1. Objects are pulled toward Earth by
   - ☐ **a.** speed.
   - ☐ **b.** gravity.
   - ☐ **c.** air resistance.

2. The force that pushes against a falling object is called
   - ☐ **a.** gravity.
   - ☐ **b.** levity.
   - ☐ **c.** air resistance.

3. Air is made up of
   - ☐ **a.** nothing.
   - ☐ **b.** only oxygen.
   - ☐ **c.** gases.

4. The speed at which an object falls depends mostly on the object's
   - ☐ **a.** shape, size, and magnetism.
   - ☐ **b.** shape, size, and weight.
   - ☐ **c.** shape, color, and weight.

5. Parachutes work by increasing
   - ☐ **a.** air resistance.
   - ☐ **b.** gravity.
   - ☐ **c.** weight.

Understanding Ideas

1. From the article, you can conclude that a leaf falls slowly from a tree because it has
   - ☐ **a.** resistance to gravity.
   - ☐ **b.** a large surface area for something that weighs so little.
   - ☐ **c.** magnetic attraction to a tree.

2. If an oak board and an oak cube of the same weight were dropped together,
   - ☐ **a.** the cube would hit the ground first.
   - ☐ **b.** the board would hit the ground first.
   - ☐ **c.** they would hit the ground at the same time.

3. The speed of an object increases as it falls, so an object dropped from higher up moves
   - ☐ **a.** more slowly than an object dropped from lower down.
   - ☐ **b.** faster than an object dropped from lower down.
   - ☐ **c.** at the same speed as an object dropped from lower down.

4. A strong upward wind probably causes objects to fall
   - ☐ **a.** faster.
   - ☐ **b.** at the same speed as they would without wind.
   - ☐ **c.** more slowly.

5. From the article, you can conclude that without air resistance all objects would fall
   - ☐ **a.** slowly.
   - ☐ **b.** at speeds different from one another.
   - ☐ **c.** at about the same speed.

C. Reading Strategies

1. Recognizing Words in Context

Find the word *usually* in the article. One definition below is closest to the meaning of that word. One definition has the opposite or nearly the opposite meaning. The remaining definition has a meaning that has nothing to do with the other two words. Label the definitions **C** for *closest*, **O** for *opposite* or *nearly opposite*, and **U** for *unrelated*.

_____ **a.** never

_____ **b.** sadly

_____ **c.** often

2. Distinguishing Fact from Opinion

Two of the statements below present *facts*, which can be proved. The other statement is an *opinion*, which expresses someone's thoughts or beliefs. Label the statements **F** for *fact* and **O** for *opinion*.

_____ **a.** Air resistance is also called drag.

_____ **b.** A parachute helps slow a person's fall through the air.

_____ **c.** People should always wear parachutes whenever they jump.

3. Making Correct Inferences

Two of the statements below are correct *inferences*, or reasonable guesses, that are based on information in the article. The other statement is an incorrect, or faulty, inference. Label the statements **C** for *correct* inference and **I** for *incorrect* inference.

_____ **a.** The force of gravity keeps people on the ground.

_____ **b.** Bowling balls are always heavier than flat pieces of plastic.

_____ **c.** A sheet of paper crumpled into a ball would have less air resistance than a sheet of paper left smooth and flat.

4. Understanding Main Ideas

One of the statements below expresses the main idea of the article. Another statement is too general, or too broad. The other explains only part of the article; it is too narrow. Label the statements **M** for *main idea*, **B** for *too broad*, and **N** for *too narrow*.

_____ **a.** Objects that are the same size, shape, and weight fall at the same speed.

_____ **b.** Gravity and air resistance are two of Earth's natural forces.

_____ **c.** Air resistance and the force of gravity affect the way objects fall to the ground.

5. Responding to the Article

Complete the following sentence in your own words:

Before reading "Gravity and Air Resistance," I already knew

_____

_____

D. Expanding Vocabulary

Content-Area Words

Cross out one word or phrase in each row that is not related to the word in dark type.

1. **gravity**	down	float	fall	pull
2. **resistance**	force	opposing	drag	oxygen
3. **speed**	map	velocity	fast	slow
4. **surface**	outside	inside	top layer	air resistance
5. **parachute**	fall	slow	air resistance	drift

Academic English

In the article "Gravity and Air Resistance," you learned that *interact* means "to work together with or communicate between." *Interact* can describe how gravity and air resistance work together. *Interact* can also describe how other things or people work together or act upon one another, as in the following sentence.

During a meeting, people interact to solve problems.

Complete the sentence below.

1. Certain chemicals *interact* to produce either good or bad _____

Now use the word *interact* in a sentence of your own.

2. _____

_____

You also learned that *utilizes* means "makes use of something." *Utilizes* can be used to describe how a parachute makes use of air resistance to slow a person's fall. *Utilizes* can also describe making use of other things, as in the following sentence.

A chef utilizes equipment such as pots, pans, and bowls.

Complete the sentence below.

3. A bird *utilizes* its wings in order to _____

Now use the word *utilizes* in two sentences of your own.

4. _____

5. _____

 Share your new sentences with a partner.

Some Spiders of North America

Before You Read

 Think about what you know. Skim the article on the opposite page. Look for information about spiders that live in your area.

Vocabulary

The content-area and academic English words below appear in "Some Spiders of North America." Read the definitions and the example sentences.

Content-Area Words

webs (webz) nests, made by spiders and some insects, of fine threads that form a design
  Example: The *webs* of a spider catch flies and other insects in their silk strings.

poisonous (poi′zə nəs) full of poison, a substance that may cause sickness or death
  Example: The deadly nightshade plant is *poisonous* to people but not to birds.

hourglass (our′glas′) a device, used to measure time, made of two clear, round glass containers connected by a thin glass tube through which sand pours
  Example: Sand moves slowly from the top to the bottom of an *hourglass*.

violin (vī′ə lin′) a musical instrument that has strings and is held on the shoulder
  Example: To make music on a *violin*, you slide a bow along its strings.

funnels (fun′əlz) cone shapes, each with a small opening at the bottom through which things are poured
  Example: *Funnels* can help you pour liquid from a large container into a small one.

Academic English

category (kat′ə gôr′ē) one part of a group, class, or type
  Example: Panthers are a *category* of large cats.

approach (ə prōch′) to move nearer to
  Example: You must stop the car when you *approach* a red light.

Do any of the words above seem related? Sort the seven vocabulary words into two or more categories. Write the words down on note cards or in a chart. Words may fit into more than one group. You may wish to work with a partner for this activity. Label one category *Devices*.

Dictionary Now skim the article and look for other words that are new to you. Write each new word and its definition in the Personal Dictionary.

While You Read

 Think about why you read. What do you know about spiders? Write a question about spiders that you would like to know the answer to. As you read, you may find the answer.

Some Spiders of North America

1 Spiders are part of a **category** of animals called arachnids. Scientists do not call spiders insects because spiders have eight legs and bodies that are split into two parts. Insects have six legs and bodies that are split into three parts. Most spiders eat insects. Many spiders catch insects in **webs** that they spin, or weave,
5 out of a sticky, smooth, stringlike material. The material, called silk, comes out of small body parts, called spinnerets, on the spider's stomach. The insects that get stuck in the webs are called the spider's prey. An animal is called prey if it is hunted or killed for food.

The wolf spider is a kind of spider that is found in many places. Most wolf
10 spiders have long legs and bodies that stay close to the ground. They do not catch their insect prey in webs. Instead, they grab their prey with their front legs and crush or chew it with their jaws. One kind of wolf spider is the trap-door spider. This spider lives in a hole in the ground that is covered by a door made of silk and dirt. The spider quickly flips open the trapdoor and grabs its prey as the prey
15 walks by. Another type of wolf spider is the tarantula. The tarantula is known for its large, hairy body.

Many people are afraid of spiders. Although all spiders are **poisonous,** their bites do not usually cause people to die. Spider venom, or poison, is most dangerous for small children and older people. In the United States, the spiders
20 with the most dangerous venom are the black widow and the brown recluse. Among black widow spiders, only adult female spiders are dangerous. They are about 4 centimeters (1½ inches) long and have a red **hourglass**-shaped mark on their black bodies. Black widows often build their webs outdoors in dark places near the ground—for example, in a pile of wood, or near the floor of a garage or a
25 small building such as a shed. Like most other spiders, black widows do not attack often. They usually bite only when someone bothers them.

The brown recluse spider is a small brown spider with long legs. It is found mostly in southern states. It likes quiet areas near the ground—for example, in the corner of a closet floor. It may hide in clothes if they are not used for a long time.
30 This spider is also called the **violin** spider because of a dark violin-shaped mark behind its eyes.

Funnel-web spiders are small with brownish-gray bodies. They build webs shaped like **funnels,** where the spider rests. In front of the funnel is a flat layer, or sheet, of web. The web traps, or catches, insects. When the spider feels
35 movements on the sheet of web, it will **approach** the moving insect and sting it. It then wraps its prey in silk and pulls it into the funnel to eat it.

LANGUAGE CONNECTION

Spider's, the possessive form of *spider,* means "of the spider." What does *the spider's stomach* mean?

CONTENT CONNECTION

The tarantula is one of the best-known spiders. It lives in the American South and Southwest, including southern California. Tarantulas can live between 25 and 40 years. They have eight eyes and can be 12 inches wide! Have you ever seen one?

After You Read

A. Organizing Ideas

What are some types of spiders? Complete the chart below. In the first box of each column, write the name of one of the types of spiders discussed in the article. Under each, list at least three facts about that type of spider. Refer to the article to help you. Some have been done for you.

Wolf Spiders	_____	_____	Funnel-Web Spiders
1. They have long legs and bodies that stay close to the ground.	1. Only the adult females are dangerous to people.	1.	1.
2.	2.	2.	2.
3.	3.	3.	3.

What makes spiders different from each other? Write two or more sentences that describe the differences. Did the chart help you understand the differences? Why or why not?

_____

_____

_____

_____

B. Comprehension Skills

Tip! **Think about how to find answers.** Look back at different parts of the text. What facts help you figure out how to complete the sentences?

Mark box **a, b,** or **c** with an **X** before the choice that best completes each sentence.

Recalling Facts

1. Spiders are
   - ☐ **a.** crustaceans.
   - ☐ **b.** arachnids.
   - ☐ **c.** insects.

2. The trap-door spider is one kind of
   - ☐ **a.** wolf spider.
   - ☐ **b.** funnel-web spider.
   - ☐ **c.** brown recluse spider.

3. One of the most poisonous spiders in the United States is the
   - ☐ **a.** trap-door spider.
   - ☐ **b.** funnel-web spider.
   - ☐ **c.** brown recluse spider.

4. A female adult black widow spider has a mark on it that looks like a
   - ☐ **a.** red hourglass.
   - ☐ **b.** black violin.
   - ☐ **c.** yellow egg.

5. Spiders have
   - ☐ **a.** four legs.
   - ☐ **b.** eight legs.
   - ☐ **c.** twelve legs.

Understanding Ideas

1. From the article, you can conclude that spiders help people by
   - ☐ **a.** staying outdoors.
   - ☐ **b.** eating pesky insects.
   - ☐ **c.** eating most mosquitoes.

2. In the South, dusty old clothes in an unused closet are likely to hide a
   - ☐ **a.** wolf spider.
   - ☐ **b.** black widow spider.
   - ☐ **c.** brown recluse spider.

3. From the article, you can conclude that if you notice a black widow spider in a web, you should
   - ☐ **a.** stay away from it and notify an adult.
   - ☐ **b.** find some matches and burn it up.
   - ☐ **c.** try immediately to kill it.

4. You can also conclude that
   - ☐ **a.** all spiders jump on their prey.
   - ☐ **b.** spiders catch prey in different ways.
   - ☐ **c.** all spiders trap their prey in webs.

5. The best way to tell one kind of spider from another is by
   - ☐ **a.** the size and marking of each.
   - ☐ **b.** the number of legs each has.
   - ☐ **c.** the type of web each one spins.

C. Reading Strategies

1. Recognizing Words in Context

Find the word *split* in the article. One definition below is closest to the meaning of that word. One definition has the opposite or nearly the opposite meaning. The remaining definition has a meaning that has nothing to do with the other two words. Label the definitions **C** for *closest*, **O** for *opposite* or *nearly opposite*, and **U** for *unrelated*.

_____ **a.** divided or cut

_____ **b.** put together

_____ **c.** mixed

2. Distinguishing Fact from Opinion

Two of the statements below present *facts,* which can be proved. The other statement is an *opinion,* which expresses someone's thoughts or beliefs. Label the statements **F** for *fact* and **O** for *opinion.*

_____ **a.** Tarantulas are scarier than black widow spiders.

_____ **b.** A spider's body is split into two parts.

_____ **c.** Many spiders spin webs from silk made by their bodies.

3. Making Correct Inferences

Two of the statements below are correct *inferences,* or reasonable guesses, that are based on information in the article. The other statement is an incorrect, or faulty, inference. Label the statements **C** for *correct* inference and **I** for *incorrect* inference.

_____ **a.** If we do not bother most spiders, they will not bother us.

_____ **b.** Making silk tires and weakens a spider.

_____ **c.** Spiders prefer dark, quiet places rather than loud, bright ones.

4. Understanding Main Ideas

One of the statements below expresses the main idea of the article. Another statement is too general, or too broad. The other explains only part of the article; it is too narrow. Label the statements **M** for *main idea,* **B** for *too broad,* and **N** for *too narrow.*

_____ **a.** Spiders share many common arachnid features but also have many differences.

_____ **b.** Black widows build webs outside in dark places, such as in piles of wood.

_____ **c.** Many kinds of spiders live in North America.

5. Responding to the Article

Complete the following sentence in your own words:

From reading "Some Spiders of North America," I have learned

_____

_____

D. Expanding Vocabulary

Content-Area Words

Complete each analogy with a word from the box. Write in the missing word.

| webs | poisonous | hourglass | violin | funnels |

1. nets : fish :: _____ : insects

2. harmless : rabbits :: _____ : spiders

3. violin : brown recluse :: _____ : black widow

4. spoons : mixing :: _____ : pouring

5. sheep : animal :: _____ : instrument

Academic English

In the article "Some Spiders of North America," you learned that *category* means "one part of a group, class, or type." *Category* can be used to describe different kinds of animals. *Category* can also be used to describe parts of other groups, classes, or types, as in the following sentence.

   Sharks are a category of fish.

Complete the sentence below.

1. My favorite *category* of books is _____

Now use the word *category* in a sentence of your own.

2. _____

   _____

You also learned that *approach* is a verb that means "to move nearer to." *Approach* can also be a noun meaning "a means of reaching a goal or getting work done," as in the following sentence.

   Playing a sport is one approach to staying healthy.

Complete the sentence below.

3. My *approach* to studying for a test is _____

Now use the word *approach* in two sentences of your own.

4. _____

5. _____

 Share your new sentences with a partner.

Talking with Instant Messaging

Read the instant-messaging conversation between Elias and Sara. Then complete the sentences. Use words from the Word Bank.

Word Bank
vapor   surface
radar   interact
capable

INSTA-CHAT

Elias: Hi, Sara.

Sara: Hi!

Elias: I had a great day today. I went on a huge sailboat with my family! It was a powerful boat, and it was _____ of carrying 75 people and reaching high speeds!

Sara: Wow! The ocean was rough today, and there was a storm. Did you feel safe in the boat even when the ocean's _____ became choppy?

Elias: Actually, our ship used _____ technology to see how far away the storm was. We saw the storm coming, so we sailed in a different direction. We did sail into some fog, though. The thick _____ made it difficult to see, but our boat crew knew what to do.

Sara: Did you learn anything about how to sail?

Elias: Sure! The crew let me help put up the sails. We had to _____ by yelling commands and replies across the boat's deck. It was very exciting! Maybe we can go sailing together sometime.

Reading an Advertisement

Read the advertisement. Circle the word that completes each sentence.

Learn to Skydive Today!

This may be the most exciting experience of your life!

- Have you ever wondered what it would feel like to fall through the sky? It would be exciting, but you would also want to feel (**external, secure**). We can teach you!

- We will train you to jump from an airplane flying at (**approximately, attract**) 10,000 feet above Earth.

Call today for your first lesson!

- You will learn how to fall safely through the air at a high (**funnels, speed**) while you enjoy the views of the landscape below.

- We will teach you to use a (**parachute, violin**) to slow your speed as you (**utilizes, approach**) the ground.

- Once you have enjoyed this amazing thrill, we are sure that you will want to skydive again and again!

 **Making Connections**

Work with a partner. Talk about what the words mean. How can you use the words to talk about a forest? List your ideas in the outline of the tree below.

greenhouse	apparent	prey	job	photosynthesis
pollination	hourglass	category	webs	poisonous

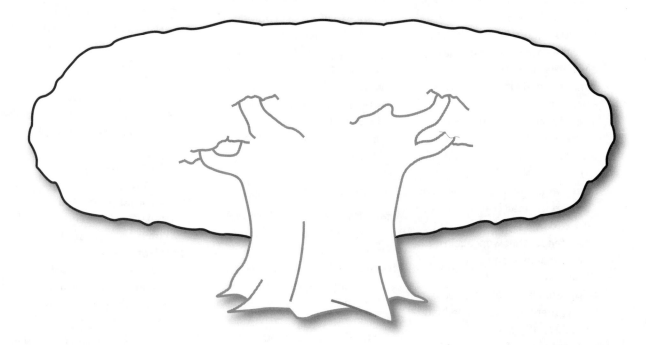

Use all of the words above in complete sentences of your own. Each sentence may include one or more of the words. To help you start writing, look at the ideas you wrote about. After you write your sentences, read them over. If you find a mistake, correct it.

_____

_____

_____

_____

_____

_____

_____

_____

_____

_____

Glossary

A

absorbs (əb sôrbz') takes in and holds or keeps without any reflection [13]

accurate (ak'yə rit) having few or no mistakes [15]

*****adequate** (ad'ə kwət) enough to meet a specific need or goal [9]

*****adjustment** (ə just'mənt) a change made in order to fix a problem [10]

*****alter** (ôl'tər) change or make different [4]

altitudes (al'tə tσσdz') heights above Earth's surface [1]

analyzes (an'əl īz'iz) examines or studies in detail [14]

antioxidants (an'tē äk'sə dənts) substances that work against the harm that oxygen can do to the body [9]

apparatus (ap'ə rat'əs) a set of equipment used for something specific [10]

*****apparent** (ə par'ənt) able to be seen [16]

*****approach** (ə prōch') to move nearer to [20]

*****approximately** (ə prok'sə mit lē) nearly or almost [16]

atmosphere (at'məs fēr') the gases or air that surrounds Earth or any other planet [12]

*****attach** (ə tach') to connect or put together [12]

attract (ə trakt') to make something come closer because of interest or feeling [18]

*****author** (ô'thər) one who writes a book or other type of literature [6]

average (av'rij) the sum of a set of values divided by the number of values [5]

B

backbones (bak'bōnz') the bones that protect the spinal cords and support the bodies of animals and people [17]

balance (bal'əns) a condition in which equal forces keep something steady, stable, or straight [4]

barrier (bar'ē ər) something that separates two areas or blocks the way [3]

bred (bred) caused to reproduce or grow [2]

C

calculations (kal'kyə lā'shənz) math work, such as addition or multiplication [1]

*****capable** (kā'pə bəl) having the ability or skill to do something [17]

carbon dioxide (kär'bən dī ok'sīd) colorless, odorless gas that people and animals breathe out [7]

carpel (kär'pel) the part of the plant that contains the seeds [18]

*****category** (kat'ə gôr'ē) one part of a group, class, or type [20]

cells (selz) the simplest units of all living things: people, animals, and plants [7]

characteristics (kar'ik tə ris'tiks) features, such as size and color, that identify someone or something [2]

civilizations (siv'ə li zā'shənz) groups of people living and working together [15]

clay (klā) a sticky material found in the earth that can be shaped when it is wet and that gets hard when it is dried or baked [11]

C

compounds (kom'poundz') mixtures or combinations of two or more ingredients [9]

conditions (kən dish'ənz) things necessary for the appearance or happening of something [11]

*****consists** (kən sists') is made (of) [5]

*****consult** (kən sult') to seek advice or ideas from someone or something [11]

continental (kon'tə nent'əl) relating to the landmasses of the seven continents, or large areas of land on Earth [5]

*****contract** (kən trakt') tighten or draw together [10]

*****cooperated** (kō op'ə rāt'əd) acted with another or others for a common purpose [1]

*****core** (kôr) the center part [5]

craters (krā'tərz) bowl-shaped holes in the ground around the opening of volcanoes [3]

crystals (krist'əlz) minerals, with patterns and flat surfaces, that are often clear and transparent [12]

currents (kur'ənts) directed flows of air, water, or electricity [12]

D

*****demonstrate** (dem'ən strāt') to show or explain by using an example [13]

devices (di vīs'əz) inventions or machines made for specific reasons [8]

dinosaurs (dī'nə sôrz') huge reptiles that lived and died out many ages ago [17]

*****display** (dis plā') show information in a way that people can see easily [8]

*****distributes** (dis trib'ūts) divides (something) among people or things [7]

---

* Academic English word

Lesson numbers appear in brackets.

document (dok′yə mənt) something written that gives important information [6]

dynamite (dī′nə mīt′) an explosive, or substance that bursts into flame easily, made with a chemical called nitroglycerin [6]

E

eardrum (ēr′drum′) a thin layer of skin that separates the parts of the ear and vibrates when sound waves reach it [14]

ecology (ē kol′ə jē) the study of the relationship between a living thing and the world around it [2]

electromagnetic (i lek′trō mag net′ik) referring to magnetic energy made by a current of electricity [13]

*__enables__ (i nā′bəlz) makes able or possible [4]

environment (en vī′rən mənt) surroundings that affect life and growth [2]

*__establish__ (es tab′lish) to build or set up [6]

*__expand__ (iks pand′) enlarge or increase in size [3]

*__external__ (iks turn′əl) located on the outside [17]

F

fertilizer (furt′əl ī′zər) nutrients added to the soil to help plants grow [11]

flexible (flek′sə bəl) able to bend and twist easily [10]

flight (flīt) the act of flying in the air [4]

forces (fôrs′iz) forms of power or energy used on an object [4]

*__function__ (fungk′shən) to work properly [9]

fund (fund) money set aside and ready for a specific purpose [6]

funnels (fun′əlz) cone shapes, each with a small opening at the bottom through which things are poured [20]

G

*__goal__ (gōl) an accomplishment toward which effort or work is directed [1]

gravity (grav′ə tē) the force that pulls objects towards the ground [19]

greenhouse (grēn′hous′) a building, made of glass or clear plastic, in which plants are grown [16]

gymnastics (jim nas′tiks) physical exercises that help someone develop strength and balance [10]

H

high-pressure (hī′ presh′ər) applying strong force from one thing to another [16]

honors (on′ərz) special credits or symbols of great respect given to people who deserve or have earned them [6]

hourglass (our′glas′) a device, used to measure time, made of two clear, round glass containers connected by a thin glass tube through which sand pours [20]

humidity (hū mid′ə tē) moisture or dampness of the air, caused by water vapor [12]

I

impairment (im pār′mənt) a problem, sometimes caused by injury, that makes it difficult or impossible to do something without help [8]

infections (in fek′shənz) illnesses or problems that result when harmful living things, such as germs, enter the body [9]

*__interact__ (in′tə rakt′) to work together with or communicate between [19]

intestine (in tes′tin) an area like a tube inside the body where food is broken down [7]

J

*__job__ (job) work that is supposed to be done [18]

K

keyboard (kē′bôrd′) an arrangement of buttons, called keys, that are used for typing [8]

L

landslides (land′slīdz′) large amounts of dirt or rocks that slide down a mountain or hill [3]

M

mantle (man′təl) the part of Earth that surrounds the central core [5]

memory (mem′ə rē) the collection, in the mind, of things learned and remembered [14]

*__methods__ (meth′ədz) ways or systems for reaching a goal [15]

minerals (min′ər əlz) things— such as gold, coal, or water— that are made by nature and are usually found in the ground [5]

---

* Academic English word

Lesson numbers appear in brackets.

moisture (mois′chər) water or other liquid in the air [12]

N

nerves (nurvz) tiny, ropelike bands of tissue that carry electrical impulses between the brain and the spinal cord and to other parts of the body [10]

*****normal** (nôr′məl) regular or usual [13]

O

orbits (ôr′bits) moves in a circle around (something) [1]

osteoporosis (os′tē ō pə rō′səs) a disease that causes weak bones [9]

oxygen (ok′sə jən) colorless, odorless gas in the air that people and animals breathe in [7]

P

parachute (par′ə sho͞ot′) an umbrella-like device used to slow down something that is falling through the air and help it land safely on the ground [19]

particles (pär′ti kəlz) tiny bits of matter that take up space and can be weighed [13]

*****perceives** (pər sēvz′) recognizes (something) through one of the senses [14]

photosynthesis (fō′tə sin′thə sis) a process through which plant cells use sunlight to make food for the plant [18]

place value (plās val′ū) the meaning or worth of a number depending on its position [15]

poisonous (poi′zə nəs) full of poison, a substance that may cause sickness or death [20]

pollen (po′lən) the powdery material that makes seeds develop [18]

pollination (po′lə nā′shən) the process by which pollen is transferred to the carpel of a flower [18]

*****potentially** (pə ten′shə lē) in a way that seems possible [12]

pressure (presh′ər) a force applied by one thing upon another [4]

prey (prā) an animal that is hunted or killed for food [17]

prism (priz′əm) a clear solid shape that breaks light up into the basic colors [13]

*****purchase** (pur′chəs) to buy [15]

pyramids (pir′ə midz′) huge stone structures that have four triangle-shaped sides that meet in a point [15]

R

radar (rā′där) a device that can identify faraway objects by means of sound waves [16]

reflects (ri flekts′) throws or gives back waves of light, heat, or sound [13]

relatives (rel′ə tivz) animals or people that come from the same family [17]

*****research** (rē′sərch′) careful search or examination [2]

resistance (rə zis′təns) an opposing force or power [19]

rocket (rok′it) a machine that burns fuel and mixes it with air to make hot gases that push it through the air [1]

roots (ro͞ots) the part of a plant that grows downward into the soil and takes in water and food [11]

S

satellite (sat′əl īt′) a vehicle that circles heavenly bodies, such as Earth or the Moon [1]

*****secure** (si kyo͞or′) kept or held firmly [18]

*****select** (si lekt′) to choose something from a group of choices [11]

sensory cortex (sen′sə rē kôr′teks) the part of the brain that relates to the senses [14]

*****shift** (shift) to change place, position, or direction [3]

signals (sig′nəlz) information sent in a way that does not rely on the voice [8]

solar system (sō′lər sis′təm) the Sun and every heavenly body that circles it [5]

species (spē′shēz) a group of living things that share certain characteristics [3]

speed (spēd) quickness of movement [19]

spring (spring) a place where water flows out of the earth [3]

springboard (spring′bôrd′) a flexible board, usually fastened to something solid at one end, that is used for jumping high in gymnastics or diving [10]

sprout (sprout) to begin to grow [11]

streamlined (strēm′līnd′) having a smooth, slim shape that can move easily and quickly through air or water [4]

*****structure** (struk′chər) something built or made up of parts [14]

sulfuric acid (sul fyo͞or′ik as′id) a powerful, oily chemical that can dissolve many solids [16]

surface (sur′fis) the outside or top layer [19]

T

taxonomy (tak son′əm ē) the organization of animals and plants into groups according to their features [2]

---

* Academic English word

Lesson numbers appear in brackets.

*technology (tek nol'ə jē) scientific knowledge or inventions that make processes simpler [8]

tissues (tish'o͞oz) groups of cells that are alike and doing the same job [7]

tokens (tō'kənz) small objects, such as coins, that are used to count or stand for something [15]

*transforms (trans fōrmz') changes the way something looks, behaves, or is built [7]

*transport (trans pôrt') carry from one place to another [2]

U

*utilizes (ū'tə līz'əz) makes use of something [19]

V

vapor (vā'pər) a substance, such as smoke or fog, that has turned into a gas that can be seen [16]

venom (ven'əm) something passed on by certain animals through a bite, causing injury or death [17]

vessels (ves'əlz) tubes, such as veins, that carry blood or other body fluids [9]

vibrates (vī'brāts) moves or shakes back and forth [14]

violin (vī'ə lin') a musical instrument that has strings and is held on the shoulder [20]

W

waves (wāvz) vibrations that move through the air without being seen [8]

webs (webz) nests, made by spiders and some insects, of fine threads that form a design [20]

will (wil) an official paper that states what should happen to a person's money or possessions after he or she dies [6]

---

* Academic English word

Lesson numbers appear in brackets.

Personal Dictionary